FOLLOWING PAGE
Church Walk in 1892, the view from Tanyard towards St Mary's Church
(from the Ray Rogers Collection).

STUR

The Story of Sturminster Newton

Sturminster Newton Museum Society
Compiled and edited by Penny Mountain

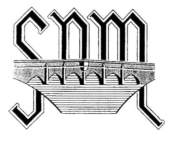

*To the people of Sturminster Newton, those born and bred here
and those from elsewhere who have chosen to make it their home.*

Stur: The Story of Sturminster Newton has been written and published by
the Sturminster Newton Museum Society. All proceeds from the sale of this
publication will be used by the Society to help maintain the Mill and
Museum and to continue to preserve the town's history. Orders to Peter
Loosmore, 16 Old Boundary Road, Shaftesbury, Dorset SP7 8ND

First published in 2006 by the Sturminster Newton Museum Society

ISBN 1 872270 05 0
ISBN 978 1 872270 05 0
EAN 9781872270050

© Sturminster Newton Museum Society 2006
The authors have asserted their rights under the Copyright, Designs
and Patent Act 1988 to be identified as authors of this work

Designed and produced by The Dovecote Press Ltd
Stanbridge, Wimborne Minster, Dorset BH21 4JD

Printed and bound in Singapore

A CIP catalogue record for this book is available from the British Library
All rights reserved

Contents

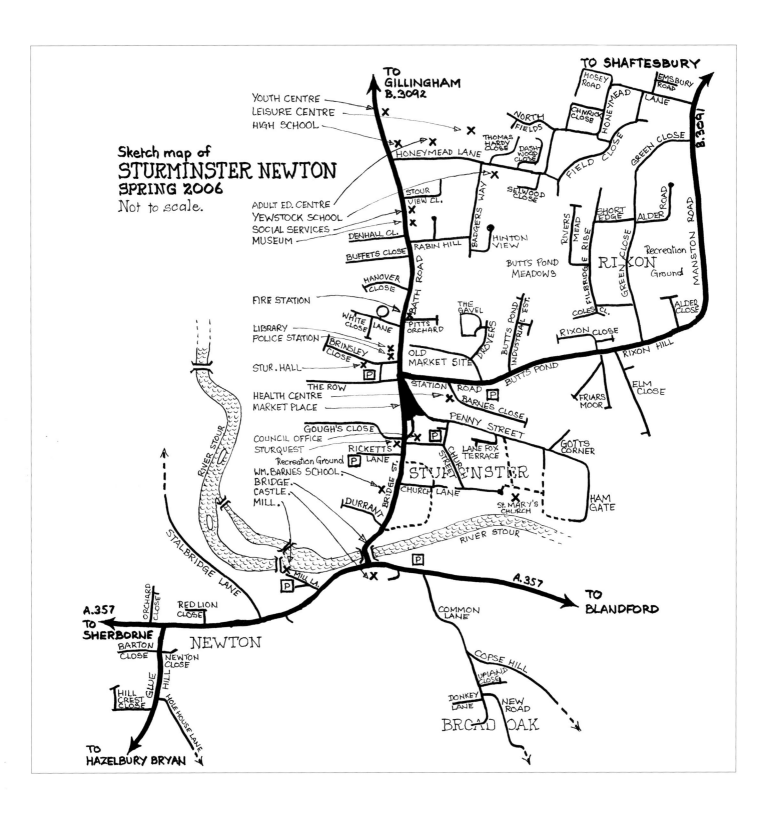

Introduction

PETER LOOSMORE
Chairman, Sturminster Newton Museum Society

THIS BOOK is published at a time when Sturminster Newton is going through huge changes. But as we look to the future we should not forget the inspiration of the past, for Stur was once a thriving and important North Dorset market town.

Fifty years ago, when I lived in Sturminster as a teenager, they said it. Thirty years ago, when I returned to this area, they said it. Twelve years ago, when I joined the Sturminster Newton Museum Society, they were saying it. And they were still saying it up until recently: 'Somebody should write a proper history of this town!'

Then, in the summer of 2004, three things happened in quick succession which inspired the Museum Society to undertake the challenge. First, we chanced upon a well-researched history of the town that the Sturminster Newton Women's Institute had compiled for a nationwide WI competition in 1983. Secondly, a letter arrived from Australia about a talented but forgotten Sturminster family of the early 20th century. Finally, Robin Ansell, Dorset County Local Studies Librarian, contacted the Museum Society to suggest that: 'Somebody should write a proper history of Sturminster Newton.'

Our title is 'story' rather than 'history' because, while striving to be historically accurate, we wanted to include anecdotes, stories and legends. We chose to use 'Stur' in the title because this is the familiar and affectionate name by which the town is known far and wide, and echoes the deep, soft tones of the old Dorset dialect.

It would be impossible to mention, particularly in a

Sturminster Newton Mill before 1926, showing the miller's cottage and in the distance Newton House.

town of this size, all the people who have made Sturminster Newton memorable, but we hope *Stur: The Story of Sturminster Newton* will give a flavour of the many different ways in which individuals, named and unnamed, have helped shape the town through the years.

So, for all of you who ever asked about the history of Stur, yer'tiz.

PETER LOOSMORE
October 2006

Foreword
The Spirit of Stur

ROGER GUTTRIDGE

IN THE SUMMER OF 1954, four months after a memorable moment in athletics history, I made my own minor contribution to the sporting life of the nation. As I was only four years old, the significance of Roger Bannister's historic four-minute mile was largely lost on me. But I remember lining up in the Recreation Ground at Stur, dressed in white shorts, running vest and plimsolls, and winning a prize for my topical impersonation of Bannister in the annual children's carnival.

Carnivals provide many of my early memories of Sturminster Newton in the 1950s and '60s, and undoubtedly contribute to the affection in which I hold the town where I spent my childhood and teenage years. There are few things that better encapsulate the 'spirit of Stur'.

Life's pleasures were simpler then, and Carnival week was an exciting time for the whole community, especially the youngsters. The climax, of course, was Carnival night, when thousands converged on the town from miles around. The crowds packed the pavements for the procession of floats, bands, cash collectors and amateur comics whose slapstick routines kept the spectators in stitches. Then it was off to Herbert's Funfair, where prices had doubled since the afternoon and fairgoers jostled and swooped in a mad scramble for a vacant bumper car or a spare seat on the switchback.

An additional attraction one year was a middle-aged stripper, who displayed her wares in a small tent as a gaggle of 15-year-old boys giggled four or five feet away. Even the artiste herself was reduced to laughter when one of our number (a visitor from 'up north') straight-facedly enquired in his Lancashire accent: 'Can we touch?' The revelations cost us a shilling each, which we considered money well spent.

Life's pleasures, as I said, were simpler then. And the market town at the heart of the Blackmore Vale was the perfect place to enjoy them. Former resident Rosemary Ellerbeck summed up the nature of the community in the prologue to her novel *The People of This Parish*, in which she used Victorian Sturminster as a model for Wenham. It was, she wrote, 'not exactly a village, not properly a town; too big for one, too small for the other'. For the outsider, it's an understandable dilemma, yet I dare say I am not the only one who has often been irritated by a certain tendency among 'townies' in the media to describe Stur as a village. To everyone who truly knows the place, it is, quite obviously, a traditional market town.

Its market traditions are much older than most people imagine, going right back to a royal charter of 1219 permitting a fair in Sturminster, the first of many charters to be granted through the Middle Ages. The arrival of the railway in 1863 provided another boost; it is no coincidence that the livestock market and Milk Factory, which were Sturminster's lifeblood for most of the 20th century, grew up within a stone's throw of the station.

There is no longer a livestock market today, but in my childhood it was the focal point of rural life. Every Monday, sleepy Sturminster came alive, its streets choked with traffic, its market areas thronged with people and stalls, its five pubs full to overflowing. In the livestock auction rooms silk-tongued auctioneers performed verbal gymnastics to tiered rows of farmers clothed almost to a man in ochre-coloured coats and flat caps.

If there is one thing for which Sturminster is more famous than its market it is its remarkable literary connections. It would be hard to find a community of comparable size that could boast of having been home to one of the great names of English literature (Thomas Hardy), two notable dialect poets (William Barnes and Robert Young, alias Rabin Hill) and a best-selling novelist of the modern era (Rosemary Ellerbeck, alias Nicola Thorne). Not to mention a handful of local literary figures, such as Olive Knott who, in my childhood, lived in Rixon Hill and wrote several books and numerous articles on Wessex history and legend. I was 17 when I knocked on her door to ask for advice on my early, tentative local history scribbles. She was most encouraging.

Despite its unusual literary connections and notable commercial past, Sturminster Newton has been a somewhat deprived community in terms of books published about it. Olive Knott and Ray Rogers went some way towards filling the gap with their anecdotal *Pictorial History*, published in 1973, while I included the pick of local photographic collections in *Blackmore Vale Camera*

Carnival 1957 watersports. Hammonds' tug-of-war team pulling for all its worth: 'In August the Stour was the venue for the river sports, a regular feature of Carnival Week in those days. Tug-of-war was the primary attraction, and with a river separating each pair of teams, it was inevitably more entertaining than its dry-land equivalent. An abiding memory is of a line of red-faced muscle-men groaning and heaving as they dug their hobnail heels into the mud and put their weight on the rope. Some pulls lasted many minutes, but once a side was broken, its members would soon be slithering into the deep in rapid succession.'
Roger Guttridge, Dorset Life (March, 1995)

in 1991. *The Marn'll Book* (1952) also contained a little Sturminster history. Yet, until now, a book of real substance about Sturminster Newton past and present has remained conspicuous by its absence. I am particularly delighted that this omission has at last been rectified and truly honoured to be invited to compose the opening words of this publication. May this ancient and interesting town prosper for generations to come!

ROGER GUTTRIDGE
September 2006

Acknowledgements

First and foremost the Museum Society is indebted to the Sturminster Newton Women's Institute who gave us permission to use their *History of Sturminster Newton*. WI members Madeleine Barber, Evelyn Bartlett, Peggy Crickmore, Queenie Gibbs, Mary Kent, Jean Miller, Sylvia Rose, Marjorie Straton and Lilian Tribe compiled the history for a nationwide competition in 1983. Without their sterling effort as a starting point and framework, *Stur: The Story of Sturminster Newton* would have been an awesome task.

As it is, the project has taken some two years and involved many hours of research and writing, time that our stalwart core of volunteer writers and editors have given generously and with good cheer.

Any fears that the project would stall at a late stage through lack of funds were allayed when an application to the National Lottery's 'Awards for All' scheme resulted in a very welcome grant of £5,000, which enabled the Museum Society to complete the work.

Researching this book has revealed surprises and delights, and some anomalies that have been passed down from source to source and into the collective memory. While we have tried to iron out the wrinkles, some truths have simply been lost in the mists of time. As far as more recent history is concerned, there are bound to be those who have a different perception of events. That's life. Over the last two years we have publicised the project and frequently asked the community to come forward with material, stories and photographs. We are very grateful to those who responded. Sadly, there was not enough space in the book to include everyone's contribution, but we would like to take this opportunity to thank all those who offered their help.

We are indebted to Penny Mountain for editing the book, to Steve Case for compiling and editing the illustrations and to the following team of writers for their chapters: Judith Bennett, Steve Case, Sylvia Denham, Felicity Harrison, Alan Harrison, John and Anne Pidgeon, Pete Loosmore, Penny Mountain and Margaret Score.

Contributions were also gratefully received from Pat Ager, Winifred Bradbury, David Cornes, Nick Curtis, David Durkin, Mary Fish, David Fox, Denise Le Voir (née Barnett), Dennis Hewitson, Pat Moody, Des O'Connor, Carol Odell, Joss Vining and the clubs and associations of the town. The help of Pat Moody, Nick Curtis and Robin Ansell in text checking and proofreading was greatly appreciated. As well as providing our foreword, Roger Guttridge and his writings have provided an invaluable source of information and we thank him for his support.

A full bibliography is given at the back of this book, but special mention should be made here of the memoirs and research of the following individuals: Reg Cluett (for his memoirs of early life in Stur), David Durkin (for his dissertation on the Iron Age Hill Fort and Manor House), the family of Ken Knott (for his memoirs of farming in the 1930s), Mary Clacy (for her thesis on the Blackmore Vale), Olive Hall (for her two books on Fiddleford), and the Revd John Day (for his booklet *Once Upon a Time in Sturminster Newton*).

For illustrations, we are particularly grateful to Gwyn Rogers for use of the Ray Rogers Collection, Margaret Score for use of the Stan Score collection, to Ann Allen, Pat Billen, David Boulton, Barry Cuff, Felicity Harrison, Jo Trowbridge and the Museum Collection. Their collections include the work of some fine local photographers, chief among them Helmut Eckardt, who has generously given us permission to use his photographs. Thanks to Mrs Kathleen

Musto for permission to use John Musto's drawings of the Mill, and to Pete Loosmore and Steve Case for their maps.

We were very pleased also to receive photographs and general assistance from: Major General and Mrs John Alexander, Graham Baseden, Michael Bean, John Billen, Blandford Museum, Richard Brown, Steve Case, Ray Castell, Roy Clarke, Stan Clarke, David and Luise Cornes, Mavis Courage, Betty Cowley, Mrs Dorothy Curtis, Jonathan Eckardt, Audrey Fox, Mrs Barbara Geary, Roger Gingell, Sylvie Guttridge, Jim and Peggy Hatcher, Dr Katrina Legg, David Lewis, Carol Lodder, Pete Loosmore,

Market Day in about 1906 with the Swan Inn on the right and the Police Station in the background.

Philip Loosmore, Muriel Moss, Lionel Mumford, National Monuments Record, Anthony Pitt-Rivers, Sylvia Rose, Arnold Trowbridge, Jo Trowbridge, David White and Rosemary Wynn.

We are also grateful for the support of retailers in the town and in particular to Philip Hart and Tony Butler.

Finally, thanks to David Burnett and Dovecote Press for holding our hand and producing such a handsome book.

ONE

Sturminster Newton Down the Ages

STURMINSTER NEWTON is a small market town in North Dorset. It straddles the River Stour at the heart of the gently rolling Blackmore Vale. Thomas Hardy described this rich agricultural area as 'the beautiful Vale of Blackmore . . . in which the fields are never brown and the springs never dry'. The town comprises two communities: Sturminster, which sits within a loop of the Stour, and Newton, a hamlet on a rise south of the river upstream from the bridge.

The Neolithic people from Europe were the first settlers and farmers in the Blackmore Vale – well before BC 3000. Archaeological finds reveal that they brought with them pottery, domesticated animals, farming and trade. Successive settlers continued to cultivate the land, and it seems likely that, as the woodlands were cleared, the area began to be covered by expanses of turf, which remained the basis of agriculture until the 19th century.

About 2,000 years ago the people of the Iron Age built a hill fort overlooking a ford across the Stour (just downstream of Town Bridge). When Vespasian's Second Augustan Legion marched in and subjugated these parts between 69 to 79 AD, the Dorset and Somerset tribe of the Durotriges was a constant thorn in the side of the Romans, leading to a military presence locally on Hod Hill. However, once the region was subdued, several centuries of prosperity followed. Evidence of local Roman occupation and settlement has been found at Marnhull, Shillingstone, Fifehead and, of course, the greatest find of all at

The Hinton Mosaic, discovered on John White's land at Hinton St Mary, is now in the British Museum. Senior pupils at the High School helped excavate the site.

An aerial view of Sturminster in 1973. Running the length of the right side of the photograph is the route of the railway line; the track has been taken up, the station demolished, but the railway cutting has not yet been filled in. Hanson's and Streeter's can be made out bottom right. Vine House Field (bottom centre) is now Barnes Close.

neighbouring Hinton St Mary – the Romano-British Mosaic (now in the British Museum), believed to be one of the earliest depictions of Christ in the UK.

With the implosion of the Roman Empire and the sacking of Rome in 410 AD, the Roman army and many settlers withdrew, ushering in a period of upheaval, inter-tribal disputes, invasion and war. The Saxons raided and by the seventh century had settled the area from Berkshire to Devon.

This period of relative peace and civilization in Wessex was shattered in the late eighth century by Viking raids, and by the time Alfred, a Saxon, became king of Wessex in 871 most of his kingdom was in pagan Danish hands. But Alfred was resourceful and dogged, and eventually forced the Danes to make peace following a decisive battle at

Proof that the Vikings did not spare Sturminster – at least during Carnival 1962.

Edington. After wresting back control of Wessex, Alfred reorganised its defences, built a network of fortified market towns – 'burhs' – and encouraged learning and religious observance. He founded the Abbey of Shaftesbury to which he granted estates in Dorset, including Hinton St Mary.

WHAT'S IN A NAME?

It is impossible to say when the name 'Sturminster Newton' was first used because early references are frustratingly ambiguous – a consequence of the community's 'split personality' perhaps. The name Sturminster is derived from Stour Minster, the 'Minster on the Stour', while Newton comes from 'new-tun', a new settlement. The etymological evidence therefore suggests that a settlement at Sturminster existed before that at Newton (though the Iron Age settlement at Newton of course predates both of these.)

Alfred died in 899 with an immense personal fortune. In his will, he bequeathed land at Sturminster to his younger son Aethelward. This bequest has often been claimed as the first mention of Sturminster Newton, but alas the reference is almost certainly to Sturminster Marshall. (Indeed there is a statue of Alfred in St Mary's Church there.)

The first identifiable reference to our Sturminster is oblique. In 968 Alfred's great grandson King Edgar gave 30 hides of land (*cassatos*) 'at Stour' to St Mary's Church at Glastonbury. There are no further details, but one might speculate about the nature of a settlement on the north bank of the Stour on two counts. First, that the gift would have included a community of sufficient size to pay tithes, and therefore be of some value; and second, that there was by this time a church (or minster) here, however modest, and that the monks in this marginal, marshy outpost might have welcomed a mother church.

At any rate, Edgar's gift was to have a lasting impact on

THE DOMESDAY BOOK ENTRY FOR NEWTON (1086)

'The Church of St Mary of Glastonbury holds Newentone. In King Edward's time it was taxed for twenty-two hides. There is land to thirty-five ploughs. Besides this land there are fourteen carucates in the demesne there which were never taxed. There are twenty-one villanes and eighteen bordars and ten cottagers there; and thirteen coliberts and fifteen bondmen. Three mills pay forty shillings, there are six acres of meadow. Wood two miles and a half long, and one mile broad. It was worth thirty pounds; now twenty-five pounds. Of the land of this manor Waleran holds six hides; Roger, one hide; Chetel, one hide. These eight hides may be tilled with eleven ploughs. They are worth seven pounds.

Of the same land, Goscelm, the cook holds four hides of the King. He has two ploughs there, and two bondmen; and five villanes and six bordars with four ploughs; and a mill which pays three shillings and nine pence; and there are sixteen acres of meadow. Wood half a mile long and one quaranten broad. It was, and is worth four pounds.'

Carucate – a measurement of land
Hide – being a standard unit in the early Middle Ages believed to represent the amount of land required to maintain a peasant and his family; between 60 and 120 acres.
Bordars and Coliberts – peasants renting land in return for services and labour.

the community. For some five centuries the Abbey and abbots of Glastonbury would control the lives spiritual and temporal of the people of Sturminster and Newton.

Newton is first mentioned in 1016 when, before his death, King Edmund 'Ironside' made an additional gift of '17 hides of Newetone Kastel' to Glastonbury. And it is 'Newentone' not Sturminster that is recorded in the Domesday survey of 1086 as belonging to Glastonbury Abbey, confirming that Newton was at least the manorial centre in this period. (While Domesday refers to manorial names it often reveals little about the settlement or the nature of the site and no mention is made of a castle or other building.)

In Edmund's gift we have also the first mention of a castle. Whether there was ever a castle in the accepted sense is a matter of debate; only archaeological excavation would confirm its existence. Yet given the site's history as an Iron Age fort and its strategic location, fortified buildings of some kind – keeps, towers, ramparts of earth, wood and stone – were undoubtedly erected, razed and rebuilt down the centuries (see below). Still standing today are the remains of a substantial 14th-century manor house that was most probably built for the steward of the Abbot of Glastonbury. Generations of Sturminster people have called this ruin 'the Castle', and indeed the town has often been recorded as Sturminster Newton Castle.

Little is known of the early history of Sturminster Newton, although in the 13th century, Michael of Ambresbury, Abbot of Glastonbury (1235 to 1252), recorded in colourful detail the duties that each of the 26 Newton tenants was expected to perform for the Fathers of Newton (on behalf of Glastonbury). He had inherited a large debt on the monastery and was trying to get its finances into shape, but his writing sheds light on medieval life here and its exacting conditions. A typical example is: 'Walter Bird has 40 acres of land and his yearly rent is 2s 7d . . . At Easter he must give to the Fathers 100 eggs and he must respond to any calls in winter time for his services as a ploughman . . . He has to cut brushwood for fuel for the Manor fires like other tenants.'

The existence of a small town by the late 13th century is suggested by a number of property transactions of the

period. The Colber family was amassing land and property and by 1317 owned a good deal of Sturminster. The Lay Subsidy of 1332 has 20 people paying 18s 3d, which might indicate a small and poor settlement, but most of the Colber holding was by now in the hands of Glastonbury which does not appear in the return, so this may not be a true reflection of the town's size.

The history of medieval Sturminster Newton is, to some extent, revealed in the growth of its market. As both the settlements of Sturminster and Newton were situated at a strategic crossing point on the river, the area was an ideal

---

TIMELINE

968 AD	King Edgar gives land 'at Stour' to Glastonbury Abbey
1016	King Edmund gives Newetone Kastele to Glastonbury
1086	Newton mentioned in Domesday Book
1219	Royal charter for fair in Sturminster
1486	St Mary's Church built by Abbot John Selwood
1539	Glastonbury Abbey dissolved
1544	Henry VIII grants Newton manor to Queen Katherine Parr
1645	Clubmen attack Roundhead garrison in Sturminster
1714	Pitt family becomes major local landowner
1729	Fire destroys centre of Sturminster
1801	First Census; population, 1,406
1817	Church School built
1825	St Mary's rebuilt by Revd Lane Fox
1832	Church Street Chapel built by Wesleyans
c. 1835	Boys School founded by Revd Lane Fox
1838	Union Workhouse opened
1863	Somerset & Dorset Railway opened
1906	Water main laid across riverbed
1913	Council School (William Barnes) built Milk Factory set up
1960	Secondary Modern School (High School) opened
1963	Roman Mosaic excavated at Hinton St Mary
1966	Somerset & Dorset Railway closed
1997	Livestock Market closed
2000	Milk Factory closed
2007	The Exchange opens

Across the river from Sturminster, between Stalbridge Lane and the River Divelish, lay a medieval farmstead, Colber. Long since abandoned, the shape of the farm can barely be made out, but in 1086, at the time of the Domesday Book, Coleberie (Colber Crib Farm) covered eight acres and was a royal manor.

Colber Crib lay within the Hundred of Newton on land that belonged to the king. The tenancy agreement, which went back to the Saxon era, described it as a 'Night's Farm', because it had to provide rest and overnight accommodation for the king, his retinue and all their horses as they travelled about the realm. (Colber Crib was one of only two such places in the area, the other being the manor of Gillingham.) The tenants of a 'Night's Farm' were exempt from the 'Forest Laws', in as much as they were permitted to take fresh food from the forest on the occasion of a royal visit.

The Dorset Lay Subsidy Roll of 1332 is the earliest complete record of people in the county who paid tax on their movables or personal property; it suggests that by this stage Colber had become a small community: Colbere had 22 tax payers; Nywton (Sturminster Newton), 20 tax payers; Henton (Hinton St Mary), 29 tax payers; and Bakebere (Bagber), 10 tax payers.

The settlement that had grown up around the original farmstead was abandoned at some stage, but not as has been mooted because of the Black Death – Colber was still paying taxes in the reigns of Edward VI and Elizabeth I. It is more likely that the community gradually ran down during the 17th century. It had certainly disappeared by 1765 when Taylor's Map of Dorset shows just a field known as Colber's. Today only the names Colber Farm and Colber Bridge remain.

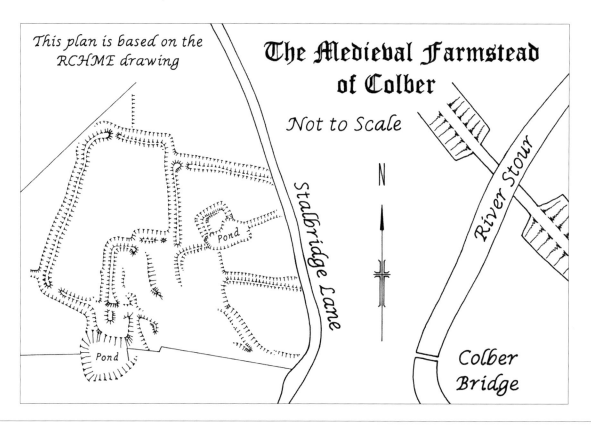

This plan is based on the RCHME drawing

The Medieval Farmstead of Colber

Not to Scale

trading centre. The earliest records of a recognised market are royal charters from Henry III, one in 1219 for a fair to be held in Sturminster and another for a fair at Newton in 1221. There is mention too of market grants being awarded in 1275 and 1278; and these were followed by a grant from Edward I for both a fair and a market in 1286. (To prevent losing the right to hold a market, which would happen if no live animals were present on market day, some livestock were kept permanently 'at the ready' nearby.) By 1332, the townships of Sturminster and Newton probably formed one administrative body as, in response to petitions by John and James Abrahams, Edward III granted rights to the manor of Sturminster Newton to hold four street fairs a year and a livestock market on days preceding the fairs.

The prosperity of the area was based on sheep and cattle rearing, so livestock formed the core of the market, which flourished to such an extent that by 1496 a petition by John Ackford for a street livestock market to be held in Sturminster Newton on one day each week was granted by Henry VII.

The reputation of the town's market was high, as indicated by a remark by Abbot John Selwood (1456-93), that 'the townlet had a very good market', and the growth of the market was mirrored in the growth of the town: 64 households were recorded in 1525, and 81 households in 1662.

Less impressed by the town was John Leland, who in 1533 received a royal commission to 'search after England's antiquities'. He wrote rather disparagingly in his 'itinerary' in around 1540: 'The townelet of Stourminstre standith in a valley, is no greate thing and the building of it is mene.' However, he liked the bridge (see Chapter 5).

The dissolution of the monasteries (1536 and 1539) and of Glastonbury Abbey in 1539 ended Sturminster Newton's long ecclesiastical connection, and the manor, lands and church living passed into the hands of the Tudor monarchs to be dealt out as gifts to various supporters, worthies and civil servants. The main landowners in this area were to become the Pitts of Stratfield-Say who took the name Pitt-Rivers when the direct line died out with George Pitt, second Lord Rivers.

STURMINSTER NEWTON CASTLE

The 'castle' site is a scheduled ancient monument lying on the south side of the River Stour, and though evidence of earlier Neolithic activity has been identified in Broad Oak, it represents the earliest settlement so far discovered in

The remains of the 14th century manor house at the Newton 'castle' site.

Clearing up after Market Day in the early 1900s. The Carpenters Arms is on the right of the picture (now Scribes).

Sturminster Newton. The site was developed in the Iron Age as a promontory hill fort. It was probably deserted by the time of the Roman invasion then re-occupied sometime in the late Saxon period and certainly by the early 11th century when the first documentary references to a 'castle' begin to appear.

The inner enclosure of the Iron Age fort is still visible as a substantial and well-preserved earthwork within the grounds of Castle Farm (now privately owned). The outer enclosure is less easily identified today, having been incorporated into a medieval field system and some time later (certainly before 1902) largely ploughed out. It can just be seen as a semi-circular earthen bank in the field beyond with a short length of ditch in the gardens of nearby Newton Farmhouse. The entrance to the fort is visible from the air. Within the inner enclosure are the much later, poorly preserved remains of the 14th-century

'rubble-built' manor house and the earthwork remains of a later rectory house and barn.

The relationship to other local Iron Age sites is unknown, but an extensive open settlement and cemetery site existed near Marnhull until destroyed by the Todber quarry. Another local hill fort is situated south of Broad Oak on Banbury Hill, and the much larger hill forts of Hambledon and Hod hills lie to the east. Two other sites (described today as 'cross dykes' on OS maps) lying across Okeford Hill and Ibberton Down, probably have Iron Age origins and were contemporary settlement areas.

The Newton hill fort was no doubt situated here because of its strategic, defensible position – high on a steep-sided triangular spur of Corallian limestone overlooking the river. The main living area was probably the inner enclosure, the outer enclosure being used for livestock. Overall the fort site occupies about two hectares. A magnetometry survey carried out in 2004 detected signs of a settlement comprising two possible Iron Age roundhouses in the grounds of Newton Farmhouse.

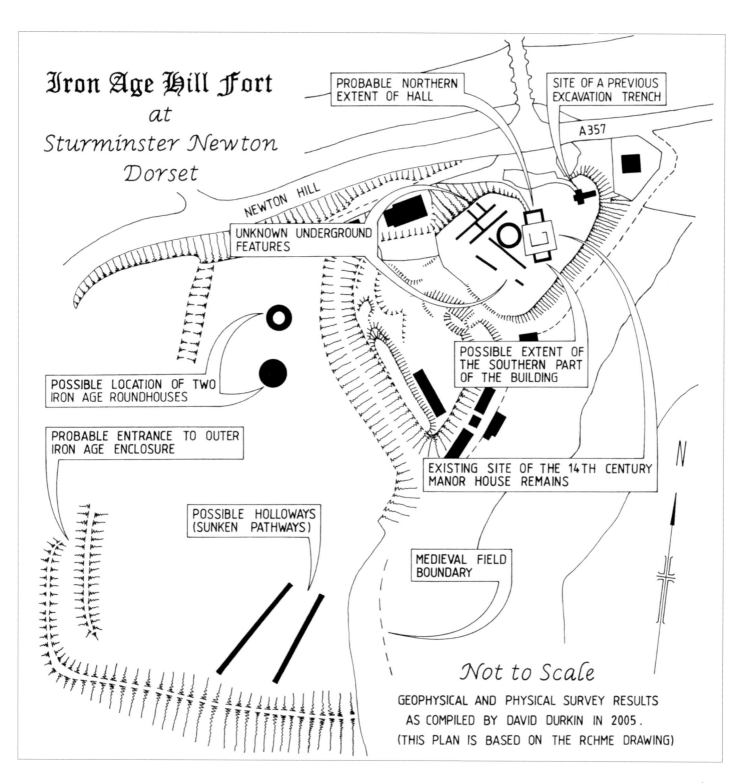

Iron Age Hill Fort
at
Sturminster Newton
Dorset

NEWTON HILL

PROBABLE NORTHERN
EXTENT OF HALL

SITE OF A PREVIOUS
EXCAVATION TRENCH

A357

UNKNOWN UNDERGROUND
FEATURES

POSSIBLE LOCATION OF TWO
IRON AGE ROUNDHOUSES

PROBABLE ENTRANCE TO OUTER
IRON AGE ENCLOSURE

POSSIBLE HOLLOWAYS
(SUNKEN PATHWAYS)

POSSIBLE EXTENT OF
THE SOUTHERN PART
OF THE BUILDING

EXISTING SITE OF THE 14TH CENTURY
MANOR HOUSE REMAINS

MEDIEVAL FIELD
BOUNDARY

N

Not to Scale

GEOPHYSICAL AND PHYSICAL SURVEY RESULTS
AS COMPILED BY DAVID DURKIN IN 2005.
(THIS PLAN IS BASED ON THE RCHME DRAWING)

Since the dissolution of the monasteries, the biggest landowner in this part of North Dorset has been the Pitt (later Pitt-Rivers) family. Edward VI gave his sister, Princess Elizabeth, the manor at Newton along with the Hundred of Newton (an ancient administrative area based on one hundred 'tuns' or villages), the rectory and the right to appoint the vicar. When Elizabeth became queen, she made several gifts within the hundred to friends and civil servants, among them Robert Freke and her Clerk of the Exchequer Sir William Pitt (whose family already owned estates in Wiltshire and Hampshire).

The properties in Sturminster Newton and Hinton St Mary in fact originated from two different ecclesiastical establishments, since the former was under the aegis of Glastonbury and the latter under that of Shaftesbury Abbey. But the Freke and Pitt estates were consolidated in the late 17th century though inheritance, when George Pitt inherited the considerable Freke estate from his aunt. His son George became the first Lord Rivers, and the family line has continued to this day for 11 generations, sometimes circuitously, though all incumbents have adopted the Pitt-Rivers name. They have been lords of the manor at Hinton St Mary since 1714 although only Anthony Pitt-Rivers, his father and grandfather have actually lived there.

Notable Pitt-Rivers have included Lieutenant General Augustus Lane-Fox Pitt-Rivers (*left*) (died 1900), who was a renowned archaeologist and anthropologist and the first Inspector of Ancient Monuments; his personal collection formed the Pitt-Rivers Museum at Oxford. (General Lane-Fox had to take the name Pitt-Rivers.) The General's son, Alexander, was the first Pitt-Rivers to live at Hinton. Alexander's son Captain George Pitt-Rivers (1890-1966), a First World War veteran, was something of a political eccentric; in 1936 he organised a march in London of 6,000 farmers and farm workers to protest against the Tithe Act, but his Mosleyite tendencies were to earn him some notoriety locally.

We should not forget here Thomas Henry Lane Fox (see Chapters 2 and 3), a nephew of the second Lord Rivers, who became vicar of St Mary's in 1839 and made Sturminster his life's work. He spent his personal fortune building schools in the town and renovating the church.

It is said that in the 19th century a man could ride from Rushmore on Cranborne Chase to Bridport without stepping off Pitt-Rivers land. An exaggeration, but when the General succeeded his cousin Horace (sixth Lord Rivers) in 1880, Augustus inherited more than 29,000 acres, made up of land at Burton Bradstock, Cerne Abbas, the family seat at Rushmore, Sturminster Newton and Hinton St Mary. Many inhabitants of Sturminster today will be living and working on land that once belonged to the Pitt-Rivers.

Down the centuries death duties and sell-offs have shrunk the estate. On the death of Captain Pitt-Rivers, the estate was divided between his sons Michael and Anthony. The latter inherited the Hinton portion of 2,000 acres along with the manor in 1970. These days the estate still includes land in and around Sturminster itself – the field at Durrant and the Mill site for example. Over the years some land has been leased out or given to the Town Council (such as the Recreation Ground). The Pitt-Rivers used to own the market site but sold it in 1958; they still own the right to hold a market in Sturminster, the proceeds of which go to the family charity.

Anthony Pitt-Rivers was High Sheriff in 1980 and served 22 years as a local councillor (non-political) on the North Dorset District Council. Mrs Valerie Pitt-Rivers became Lord Lieutenant of Dorset in 2006.

We cannot be certain whether the first historical reference to a castle, in Edmund Ironside's 1016 gift to Glastonbury, constituted a building or just referred to the area of the Iron Age fort. It has been suggested that buildings did, in fact, exist here and that these were demolished by three Dorset landowners – Robert Earl of Gloucester, William de Mohun and William de Cahaignes – to make way for an unauthorised castle they built during the Civil War of 1135-1154 between Stephen and Matilda. In *Wessex from 1000 AD*, J.H. Bettey places a castle firmly on the Stour at Sturminster in a map of 'Major medieval castles'. Leland in the 1540s, Camden in 1607 and Coker in the mid-17th century all make reference to a ruinous 'castle' (although they could be talking about the 14th-century manor).

Topographically, the most likely location of any castle is south of the existing ruin, just inside the ramparts of the Iron Age fort. Early castles were often timber constructions and were usually rebuilt several times, so an absence of remains is not surprising.

Whatever existed on the site became important in the 13th century, being favoured by King John, who stayed there on 27th June 1204, 3rd February 1207, 9th to 11th September 1207, 25th to 28th September 1208, 31st September 1213 and 3rd and 4th December 1214. Edward I was also at 'Cerminstr castle Neuton' on 30th December 1275. Why the place was so popular is not recorded, but King John is thought to have enjoyed the local hunting, and the monarchy in the Middle Ages was somewhat peripatetic. Heavy fighting during the Wars of the Roses (1455-1485) is alleged to have destroyed any castle extant at that time.

In 1544, following the dissolution of the monasteries, Henry VIII gave the site as a dowry to his queen Katherine Parr. The certificate of the lands of Glastonbury Abbey records thus: 'The scite of the said house standeth upon a high hill, just by a great running river in the valley. It is of th'auncyent building, portly and strong, able and mete for a knight to lye in. The demaynes belonging unto the same are of the yerely value of £13 6s 8d.' Queen Katherine is credited with building a new manor house in the old castle grounds, but she is far more likely to have given the existing 14th-century manor an extensive Tudor makeover.

Subsequently, Edward VI gave the manor to his sister Princess Elizabeth in 1551. Elizabeth, when queen, gave it to her courtier (and alleged lover) Sir Christopher Hatton in 1571, who leased the property the following year to Robert Freke. (The acquisitive Freke family would be described these days as 'upwardly mobile'.) In this way the site and attached lands came, by way of marriage and inheritance, through the Freke family to the Pitt family in 1714. (Sir Christopher Hatton was one of the backers of Francis Drake's voyage around the world (1577-80) and Drake renamed his ship *The Pelican, The Golden Hind*, a golden hind forming part of his patron Hatton's coat of arms.)

An 1860s edition of John Hutchins' *The History and Antiquaries of the County of Dorset* records another old building on the site, called 'Coombs', described as a small rectory house with its glebe (being the land given to the rector). Adjoining this house were the remains of a barn, dating back to around 1370, largely demolished in 1732 and completely demolished in 1840. This house was probably just below the possible castle site and on the western side of the combe, at its top; the glebe may well have been a part of the land within the combe. The stream in the combe appears to have been dammed at some stage, perhaps to form fishponds in the medieval period.

The 'castle' site and its surrounding land were owned by the Rivers Estate until about 1980. They are still in private hands.

STURMINSTER NEWTON MILL

The mill, which remains the property of the Rivers Estate, is Sturminster Newton's pride and joy, a popular North Dorset beauty spot visited by thousands every year. The mill site represents some thousand years of continuous working history. It is recorded in the Domesday survey of 1086, but a mill probably existed here long before that. The Romans are generally believed to have introduced the technology of water power to Britain.

King Edmund's bequest to Glastonbury Abbey in 1016 may well have included the mill as it certainly belonged to the abbey by 1086. By the 1230s a man known as Leuric was the tenant miller and was paying 16 shillings a year in rent plus 20 sticks of eels (a stick of eels being, quite literally, a stick with perhaps a dozen hooks on it and an eel hung on each hook).

Mill customers paid a double toll: the abbey took some of their grain and the miller an additional amount as payment. To be sure that he did not lose out on his tolls,

Sturminster miller Harry Elkins in the early 1930s. Harry Elkins was born in Broad Oak in 1879 and went to work at the mill at the age of 15. A few years later he served an apprenticeship in a Devonshire mill, returning to Sturminster in 1904. Recorded inside the lid of the miller's desk is the handwritten inscription: 'Harry Elkins 1894, Aug. 23, 1904 Came Back'. As a manufacturer of food for both humans and animals, he was forbidden to volunteer for service in the Great War (one keen young local woman presented him with a white feather). He remained at the mill all his working life, retiring in 1946 by which time the flour dust had taken its toll on his health. He died in 1949, and was succeeded by his nephew Sam Elkins, who continued to work the mill until its closure in 1970.

The mill: meal or ground floor (drawing by John Musto).

the abbot is reputed to have sent his monks out to smash or confiscate querns, the small hand-operated stones used within households. As Chaucer suggests in his *Canterbury Tales*, millers were not known for their honesty, and indeed the miller at Sturminster in 1547, Richard Whyffyn, was fined sixpence for taking excessive toll.

Over the centuries Sturminster Mill will have been rebuilt a number of times. It would have started life as little more than a timber and thatch shack with a single pair of stones powered by a horizontal wheel, and then developed step by step into a three-floored stone building housing a more powerful upright wheel with gears to drive several sets of millstones, a hoist and auxiliary machines.

The dissolution of the monasteries saw the mill (and the Fiddleford and Cutt mills) returned to the local landowner, although the estate usually leased it to professional millers; today it is leased to the Town Council.

A deed in the county archives mentions the date 1611 and 'a recently built tucking or fulling mill next to John Young's grist mill' at Sturminster Newton. This refers to the brick-built part of the mill set on a stone base and

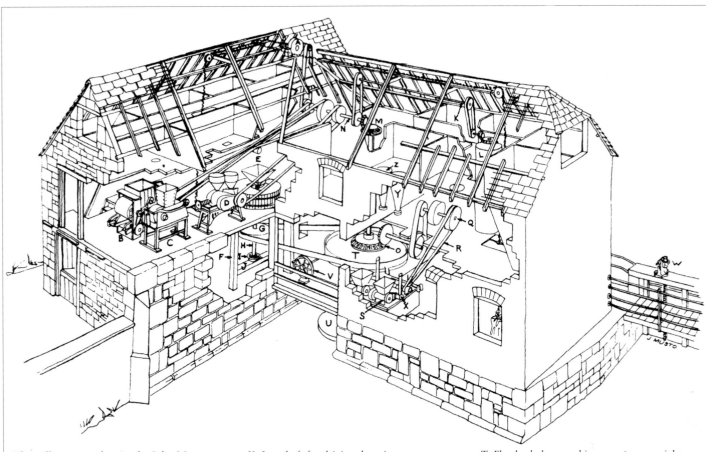

The mill: cutaway drawing by John Musto:
A Sack hoist
B Winnowing machine
C Modern crusher or roller
D Combined crusher and plate mill
E The millstones and millstone furniture
F Wooden hursting supports millstones
G Drive pulley for millstones
H Stone spindle
I Tentering wheel for adjusting gap between stones
J Hurst frame cross tree

K Lay shaft for driving the mixer
L The mixer
M Crown wheel with 48 cogs for driving line shaft
N Line shaft driven by a pinion with 16 cogs
O Crown wheel for hammer mill primary drive
P Pinion shaft for hammer mills drive
Q Lay shaft for secondary drive, for hammer mill
R Final drive for hammer mills
S Christy Norris hammer mills installed in 1947 by Armfield

T Flywheel above turbine 2.196 tons weight
U Armfield patent Empire River reaction turbine
V Pentstock sluice for controlling water to turbine
W Hatches for controlling level of head water
X Meal pipe; hammer mills blow meal into sacks
Y Bagging off points from hammer mills
Z Cyclonic dust collectors from hammer mill.

jutting out into the river. In its original form it was probably a separate stone building, but at some time this was demolished, rebuilt in brick and joined to the other mill. A local tithe map of 1783 appears to show the two mills already joined as they are now.

A fulling mill, as described above, used a waterwheel to operate heavy wooden hammers which beat ready-woven wool cloth as part of the finishing process in making a fabric such as Swanskin (see Chapters 7 and 11). The main part of the mill is the stone-built section planted firmly on

When floodwater swept away the weir in the winter of 1926-27, material from the miller's cottage was used to rebuild it.

the river bank. Experts agree that this was largely rebuilt about 1650, but there is some debate over how much of an earlier construction has been incorporated into it.

This present building is of a traditional small mill layout, comprising three floors. Grain brought to the mill in two and a quarter hundredweight sacks was hoisted to the top floor, where large bins could store up to 60 tons. From the bins it dribbled down into a winnower or rollers or mill-stones on the middle floor, and the product from these machines fell into sacks on the bottom floor. If, for example, wheat was dropped through the winnower to be cleaned, it would then have to be hoisted back to the top floor to be dropped through the stones to be ground into flour.

The hatches and rolling bay (sluice gates and weir respectively) hold back a head of water approximately four feet nine inches (one and a half metres) high, which for centuries drove a single undershot waterwheel. A second wheel was introduced alongside the first when the fulling mill was erected and this arrangement drove the mills until 1904. The last wheels were built by William Munden of Ringwood.

By 1900 Munden's successor, J.J. Armfield, had pushed the company to the forefront of hydro-technology – making water turbines. This was at a time when small rural mills were being by-passed by the railway system, stationary steam power and improving roads. In order to

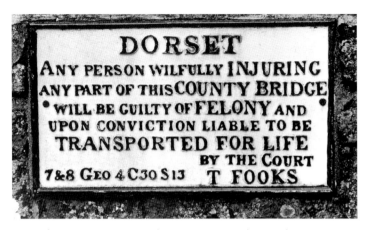

One of Dorset's rare original transportation plaques, but no one was ever transported for damaging the bridge.

compete, Sidney Knott, the mill's master miller ordered a water turbine, and in 1904 a 24 horsepower, 45 inch 'British Empire' double turbine was installed giving twice the power produced by the waterwheels. Many mills throughout the country installed turbines, but most, through neglect or demand for scrap iron, have long since disappeared, so such an original machine in full working order as Sturminster's is now much rarer than a wheel.

A miller's cottage once stood where the present car park and picnic area join but a surge of floodwater in the winter of 1926-27 swept away the rolling bay, and the cottage was demolished to provide stone for rebuilding.

From 1925 until its closure as a full-time working mill in 1970, Sturminster Mill was leased to Blandford & Webb Ltd, corn and seed merchants, who used the building to produce animal feeds from a variety of grain types. Throughout the 1980s it was administered by a Mill Trust; the millers were Bryan Young and Mrs Kathleen Musto. Tightening hygiene regulations then forced the mill to cease production, Chris Ayers being the trust's last supervisor.

Although much is known about the mill, there are mysteries yet to solve. Tithe maps of 1783 and 1853 show an addition to the building where the path now runs between the side of the mill and the car park, and at the same place a curved furrow about three feet long is gouged into the mill wall. Was there once a waterwheel on this side of the building? Why are some windows at floor level

blocked up – have the floor levels been changed? What is the significance of the large stone lintel inside the back door at fireplace level when there is no trace of a chimney in the wall or outside? A photograph of 1883 in Jo Draper's *Thomas Hardy: A Life in Pictures* shows a thatched wooden shed at the same level as the front of the mill but set back deeply into what is now the bank of the car park. What purpose did this building serve?

Sturminster Newton Mill is a particularly fine old building on an ancient site, in a beautiful setting and driven by a rare machine. This combination makes it truly unique.

THE CIVIL WAR IN STURMINSTER NEWTON

With the exception of Sherborne, which was captured by Parliamentary forces in 1642 and retaken for King Charles I in 1643, this part of North Dorset remained comparatively quiet during the early years of the English Civil War (1642-49), though no doubt some hot debates took place and a few may have joined the respective sides.

The main problem for local people seems to have been the quartering of soldiers and the 'requisitioning' of goods by both Parliamentary forces and Royalists, for which worthless chits were given. Nicholas Goffe, who farmed in Sturminster, suffered so much from taxes and losses by quartering that, to avoid imprisonment, he was forced to serve in the Parliamentary army for a year. Around the same time (1643), John Payne, waggonmaster to the King's nephew, Prince Maurice, provided release passes for 23 local farmers who had been pressed into the Royalist army.

The effective turning point of the war was the King's defeat on 4th July 1644 at Marston Moor just outside York. This defeat lost Charles the North of England, leaving the West as his main area of support. From then on, the Blackmore Vale played an increasing part in the later stages of the war.

It was against this background that Charles visited Stalbridge on 8th October 1644 and stayed at the home of Richard Boyle, first Earl of Cork. Meanwhile Prince Maurice arrived in Sturminster Newton with a detachment of troops. On the following day, Charles travelled to Blandford, picnicking on the way in a field at Sturminster before meeting up with Prince Maurice on Durweston

One might not instantly associate Sturminster with smuggling, but there is little doubt the area was once rife with it. In 1719, according to Philip Taylor, Collector of the Customs at Weymouth, 'Blackmore Vale is the most disaffected part of this county abounding in a great number of rogues.'

The earliest reported incident in Sturminster was in 1681 when Thomas Barney, the Surveyor of Customs at Poole and a man known to be corrupt, visited the town with two of his men, John Penny and Thomas Keeping. They came to search the house of a certain Mr Stephens, where they discovered five packs of cloth. Far from put out, Mr Stephens invited Barney and Penny to have a drink. The two men emerged the worst for wear and loaded the cloth on to their horses. At this point Barney began abusing and striking out at some locals, and during the fracas the cloth disappeared. Later, Keeping reported that he thought the disturbance had been caused deliberately so that the cloth might be spirited away.

No story about smuggling in this area would be complete without mentioning Roger Ridout of Okeford Fitzpaine. He and his gang of smugglers would collect their goods from the Purbeck coast and hide them around Fiddleford until it was safe to move them on. Sturminster market was one of many places where such booty was offloaded. Roger Ridout's horse, known as 'Ridout's Stumpted [or Ratted] Tail', was almost as well known as his master. There had always been rivalry between Okeford Fitzpaine and Sturminster Newton, and on one occasion when Ridout arrived in Stur people tried to force him from his saddle. Ridout apparently said to the animal,

Fiddleford Mill

'What would'ee do fer thy king?' at which the horse reared up and kicked out with such force that it broke down a door in Bridge Street. It was also rumoured that Ridout had 'bought' the silence of the local magistrate, since it was not unknown for a keg of brandy to be left on the doorstep of Vine House in Penny Street during the night.

Tales of smugglers usually involve secret tunnels. There is reputed to be a false grave in St Mary's churchyard that is the hidden entrance to a smugglers' tunnel running all the way to Okeford Fitzpaine. Another tunnel is said to link the Mill and the site of Sturminster Castle and to have been used for storing brandy after the barrels had been transported up the River Stour.

Bridge, Maurice having left a small detachment of troops to garrison Sturminster under Colonel Radford.

Towards the end of the year, Parliament had begun to get the upper hand and in November 1644, Sir Anthony Ashley Cooper took possession of the town – Colonel Radford having evacuated Sturminster without a fight – and for the remainder of the war the town was controlled by Parliament.

The quartering of troops and plundering of crops and cattle led to a movement known as the Clubmen, which consisted mainly of poor rural workers, but also a good number of clergy, farmers and minor gentry. Thomas

Sydenham, a Parliamentary officer, described them as 'a disorderly rabble and rude company of mongrel malignants and rotten hearted, nauseous neutrals'. However, the Parliamentary General Sir Thomas Fairfax considered them to be a threat to his lines of communication, especially as he was planning the siege of Sherborne Castle, held for the King by Sir Lewis Dyves.

A petition on behalf of the Clubmen, drawn up by Thomas Young, a lawyer, was totally rejected by Sir Thomas Fairfax. On 3rd July 1645, the local Clubmen attacked the Roundhead garrison in Sturminster Newton and, after a brief fight, drove them out, several being killed on both sides. Further disturbances locally convinced Fairfax that the Clubmen were a serious threat, so when he heard of a large gathering at Shaftesbury on 3rd August, he sent Oliver Cromwell (at that time second in command to Fairfax) with a detachment of about a thousand cavalry to disperse them, which Cromwell did successfully.

On the following day, Cromwell was informed of a further gathering of about two thousand on Hambledon Hill. Twice he sent emissaries to parley and on both occasions they were fired on. In a letter to Parliament, Cromwell himself describes what happened next: 'Whereupon Major Desborough wheeled about, got into the rear of them, beat them from the work and did some execution upon them. I believe killed not twelve of them but cut very many. We have taken about three hundred many of which are poor silly creatures, whom if you please to let me send them home, they promise to be dutiful for time to come, and will be hanged ere they come out again.'

After the skirmish, 16 Roundhead prisoners were released and the Clubmen taken prisoner were locked in Shroton church. Among the prisoners were Richard Burbage, son of the attorney in Sturminster, Thomas Young and John Pope from Marnhull, 'a notable malignant'. Most were released the following day but the ringleaders were sent to London.

The role of the Clubmen has been underestimated, but Joshua Sprigg, chaplain to Fairfax, was in no doubt of

The Barnett clan gather in the garden behind the shop, T.W. Barnett's, for a wedding party on 5th June 1911. Arthur Barnett and (Winifred) Mabel Cake, daughter of Sturminster grocer Charles Cake were married at the Wesleyan Chapel in Church Street. Top far left is Arthur's brother Leonard next to his father Thomas W. Barnett. His father, Edward William Barnett (aged 90, a former tailor), is sitting behind the bride. The grapevine in the greenhouse behind the shop was still producing sweet white grapes right up to the time of Barnett's fire in 1972.

ABOVE An attractive corner from bygone days. The cottages were knocked down to make way for the bungalow set back from the Blandford road just below Town Bridge.

LEFT Modest dwellings at Gotts Corner (since demolished).

their importance. 'If they had not been crushed in the egg, it had on an instant run all over the kingdom and might have been destructive to the Parliament.' Now, it was possible to travel between Salisbury and Sherborne without hindrance, so Fairfax could carry out the siege of Sherborne Castle in earnest.

The aftermath of the episode was felt later, when, in 1646, Richard Swayne, the vicar of St Mary's was turned out and replaced by Thomas Branker, a Puritan, who is listed in the church as an 'Intruder'. He was followed by John Duperier, who was also listed as such. The status quo was not restored until 1668, when Hamnet Ward, who had been a Royalist, became vicar. He remained until 1708, by which time the Civil War was but a memory.

STURMINSTER NEWTON IN 1801

The life of the common people has been hard throughout the history of North Dorset, particularly on the farms. Much of the work was done by hand and in all weathers, and farm labourers' wages were lower here than in other parts of the country. People lived in wretched conditions, and their poor health together with increasing mechanisation brought them to breaking point and to the poorhouse.

The outbreak of the French Revolutionary Wars in 1793 brought wealth to some but aggravated conditions in rural areas, which were already suffering from the increasing number of Enclosure Acts. Various schemes for Poor Relief were tried, but critics argued that they encouraged the poor to have larger families in order to obtain more money.

Celebrating Empire Day (Queen Victoria's birthday, 24th May) in the early 1900s. (In 1958 it was renamed Commonwealth Day.)

There were predictions of dire consequences if the population continued to rise.

By 1799 the government was sufficiently alarmed at the vast expenditure on Poor Relief to decide that something should be done, but the real problem was that no one knew the full extent of the population increase. Attempts at population surveys had been made from time to time since the Domesday Survey of 1086; for example, Gregory King in the 1690s used Parish Registers to calculate that the population of England and Wales was then just under six million. But a more detailed and reliable survey was now needed.

The government appointed John Rickman to carry out a full census to determine the exact number and status of the population. The Census of 1801, carried out in each parish, listed every household, dividing the occupants under the headings of male, female and listing their various occupations. The results of the census showed that the population of England and Wales was 9.2 million – a rise on Gregory King's 1690s estimate of more than 50 per cent in a hundred years.

What did the census tell us about the population in Sturminster Newton in 1801? The most common names were: Eyers, Foot, Robbets, Ridout, Yeatman, Knott, Clark, Fudge, Newman, Inkpen, Gass, Score, Harris, Jeans, Rose, Cross, Goff, Shepherd, Fish, Carter, Porter, Fuzell, Penny, Butt, Phillips, Guy and Cluett.

There were 308 households (including the poorhouse) and 1,406 inhabitants, of whom 619 were male and 787 female, about 700 of them children. Many of the adults, 283, were employed in the cloth industry – 221, all of them women, were spinners. The records show 53 weavers (only one of them a woman), 19 shoemakers, 18 butchers, 13 manuta (or shawl) makers, one breeches maker and 50 residents in the poorhouse most of whom were employed

Nostalgic reflections: Bude (eng. no. 43006) and Biggin Hill (34057) crossing the Stour over Bridge 171 towards Sturminster in March 1966.

in the wool trade. There were 12 schoolteachers, three doctors, one attorney, two millers and one beggar

Poverty continued to be rampant in the 19th century. The Sturminster poet Robert Young in his memoirs tells of labourers working from six in the morning to six in the evening. A married man received 7s (seven shillings) a week and an unmarried man 6s; bread was dear and tea was 6s a pound. Women and children picked over the fields for grain and beans; wheat and barley were ground at the mill and made into bread and barley cakes; the beans were roasted, ground and used in place of tea.

The low wages of the agricultural workers in Dorset led to union activity further south in Tolpuddle in 1834. Lord Ashley, son of the sixth Earl of Shaftesbury was so concerned at the poverty of the Dorset labourer and the squalor in which he lived that in 1843 he spoke out at a meeting of landowners and farmers held at Sturminster. He called upon them to accept 'an abatement of luxuries, a curtailing of what even are called comforts' in order that they might raise the labourers' wages and improve their housing. When he succeeded his father, he replaced many of the tumble-down hovels with decent cottages.

For some centuries a risky alternative to poverty had presented itself to the young and adventurous men of Dorset. From 1497, when John Cabot made landfall in Newfoundland, a great trade in cod steadily built up, reaching its peak in the 1700s. Huge fleets plied the North Atlantic, fishing the cod banks, running supplies and trading in salt cod in a triangle between Dorset ports (Poole in particular), Newfoundland and Europe. Rural Dorset supplied the men, its markets provisioned the voyages and the Newfoundland settlers, and a locally produced cloth, Swanskin, kept the sailors and fishermen warm and provided employment for an army of spinners and weavers back home. Men and boys as young as 10 would be recruited at hiring fairs in Sturminster and Wimborne. Some would perish on the high seas, some would return and some would settle in Newfoundland.

THE MARKET IN THE 20TH CENTURY

The single most beneficial factor for the town in the last 200 or so years was the arrival of the railway in Sturminster in 1863. This opened up huge new possibilities both for the market and for the town (see Chapter 7). As a result the livestock market flourished and grew until, in 1906, it made a much-needed transfer to a purpose-built site north of the railway, centred around the old Corn Exchange building.

The market remained open throughout the Second World War, though it was held weekly, and according to valuer and auctioneer Archie Meaker, livestock was not auctioned but graded for sale by a panel of experts. The market trebled in size after the war, expanding to cover more than seven acres; the number of animals handled increased from 23,000 in 1947 to 79,000 in 1961

By 1962, Sturminster Newton was a thriving and prosperous market town, but its prosperity was based almost entirely on the success of the livestock market and of the Milk Factory, which made it a centre for agricultural suppliers and legal and financial services.

In the years after its move to Station Road, the ownership, lease and operation of the market site were in the hands of different groups of people. In 1906 Alexander Pitt-Rivers owned the site and leased it to Harry Senior, auctioneer and estate agent. Harry Senior was later joined by George Godwin and, as Senior & Godwin, they

By 1906 the livestock market had outgrown the centre of town and was moved to a purpose-built site north of the railway line.

operated the Sturminster Livestock Market until 1986. In 1986 Senior & Godwin were bought out by Prudential Property Services, which ran the market until 1990 when the lease on the site expired. Although Prudential tried to get the lease renewed by the new owners (see below), the application was too late. A consortium, which included the partners of Senior & Godwin, took over the running of the market and, as Premier Livestock Auctions Ltd, managed the market until its closure in 1997.

During these years the ownership of the site itself changed hands. In September 1958 Captain George Pitt-Rivers sold it to Edwin Ingram; by 1975 it had passed into the ownership of Harold Senior Ingram, Edwin's son.

In 1989, a town meeting of 300 people voted to add £20 a year to their individual parish tax to buy the site from Harold Ingram, but the Town Council was unable to proceed, and that year Ingram sold the site to Speriam Holdings, a Caribbean Virgin Isles company, for £672,500 (the company later changed its name to Sturminster Holdings Ltd).

The livestock market site was advertised by estate agents Humberts as having 'redevelopment potential for commercial and residential purposes'. Redevelopment was, however, delayed, mainly because of the possible existence

Senior & Godwin's retirement party in July 1969 for Hector Beale, who started at the firm in 1915 as an office boy and retired as chief accountant. (1) Isobel James, (2) Margaret Mason, (3) Sandra Vining, (4) Mr Richards, (5) Mr White, (6) Mrs Chubb, (7) Vic Cowell, (8) Ben James, (9) Ron Weston, (10) Jean Shute, (11) Stan Thurstans, (12) Cis Fish, (13) Paul Lewis, (14) Archie Meaker, (15) Margaret Lewis, (16) David Shute, (17) Don Wootten, (18) Clive Dickinson, (19) Irene Moores, (20) Mrs Barnes, (21) Audrey Rigg, (22) Miss Beachem, (23) Mrs House, (24) Joyce Stacey, (25) Eve King, (26) Jill Loader, (27) Ted Avery, (28) Philip Loosmore, (29) Billy Bogan, (30) Betty Baker, (31) Mr E. Hibberd, (32) Mrs Meaker, (33) Hector Beale, (34) Mr Donaldson, (35) Mr Hayward.

of strips of land ('ransom strips') bordering Station Road, which would restrict access to the site. It was alleged that the strips were owned by a trust, the trustees of which refused to sell. In the meantime the market continued to operate on the site with a series of short-term leases and in an atmosphere of great uncertainty. The situation was not resolved until 1997 when the High Court ruled that the ransom strips had never existed. The market was closed a month after the ruling. The market bell rang for the last time on Monday 28th June.

The closure was a great emotional and social blow to the town as well as a commercial loss. Livestock sales, which had peaked at 100,000 animals in the 1980s, were transferred to Yeovil and Frome; the farmers, dealers and friends from the surrounding area lost their meeting place.

There had been vigorous activity by the townspeople and the town and district councils to save the livestock market. The Sturminster Market Action Group (SMAG) was formed and North Dorset District Council drew up plans that would allow some development of the site with the retention of a livestock market. Indeed, in 1994 NDDC was in a position to buy the market but was hampered by

ABOVE The winter of 1962-63 was so hard that the River Stour froze over, and the townsfolk barbecued, skated and danced on the 19-inch thick ice under floodlights. Dennis Barnett (centre) roasts a hindquarter of beef.

BELOW Sledging on the frozen Stour: Ian Lewis, Joan Luck, Ann Allen and Yvonne Lewis.

gained popularity for a time. A 'planning for real' exercise saw 500 local people giving their views on development in the town.

In 2002 a Community Task Force was consolidated as SturQuest, a 'not for profit company' run by the community. Its main purpose was to ensure that the development of the market site would include not just housing but a large community centre for the town; efforts to revive a livestock market had ceased by this stage. After

Town Crier Kevin Knapp in full cry continues the tradition of previous Town Criers Thomas and Herbert Inkpen in the 19th and 20th centuries.

the ransom strip issue. By the time this matter had been resolved, the price asked was above the council's limit set by the district valuer.

The concept of long-term planning for the future of the town was taken up by a community group calling itself Sturminster Newton 2000 & Beyond, and several proposals for the development of the market site were produced, among them a plan for an Ecology Centre that

The Grant of Arms was presented to the Rural District of Sturminster on 24th May 1962. The green field of the shield symbolises the pastures of the district, the wavy saltire (white for the milk that is the main product) represents the Rivers Stour and Lyddon, the crosses are the local mills and the sheaves are the grist for the mills. Five bulls heads (a reminder of the Cattle Breeding Centre) are set in rayed rings representing local hill forts. The mythical creature atop is apparently defending its black moor. The Latin motto means 'Who's afeared?'.

consultation with architects Phillip Proctor and developer Charles Higgins, a plan was put forward which NDDC approved in 2003. The plan for the community centre encompasses a new hall, social centre, medical centre and supermarket. In tribute to the Corn Exchange, which was the centre of the old livestock market, the community centre has been named 'The Exchange'.

There is no doubt that Sturminster Newton would have been at its most bustling and vibrant in the 'railway' years, when access to the outside world for both industry and pleasure was at its easiest and the market at its busiest. The closure of the railway and subsequently of the Livestock Market and Milk Factory were tragedies for the town. Nevertheless it has not led to the complete disappearance of Market Day. Activity focuses every Monday in the

Elections in Sturminster in the early 1900s were crowd-pullers (although women did not get the vote until 1918): the declaration of the poll at the Boys School in 1906 when Mr A.W. Wills retained his seat (won in a by-election in 1905) as Liberal MP for North Dorset.

Market Place when the centre is full of stallholders, and once a month when a Farmers' Market comes to town. The annual Cheese Festival, inaugurated quite recently but already an established and expanding event, is a reminder of the fine cheeses once produced at the Milk Factory. Meanwhile, the wealth of other activities that take place in and around the town suggests that Sturminster folk do not easily have the stuffing knocked out of them.

TWO

Believing and Seeing
Religion in Sturminster Newton

EXCAVATIONS of the Roman villa at Hinton St Mary in 1963 revealed the earliest positive indication of Christian practices in the vicinity, since the remarkable tessellated pavement bears the Christian Chi Ro symbol. (The mosaic is now in the British Museum, but an image of it is in the Sturminster Newton Museum.) No doubt pagan practices persisted, but Christianity murmured on through Viking raids and wars, for Sturminster was well within Wessex, the kingdom of the Christian King Alfred.

As noted in Chapter 1, Sturminster Newton's close link with Glastonbury Abbey, one of the most illustrious and wealthiest religious houses in England, began in 968 when King Edgar conferred 30 hides at Stour upon the abbey. From Glastonbury, a group of priests would have served the religious needs of the people of a fairly wide area, as well as collecting dues (payable in cash, kind and service). No remains have been found in Sturminster of churches of this early time, but some structure, probably wooden, would have existed.

In 1269 Glastonbury Abbey appropriated the living of Sturminster to boost its resources in a period of economic decline, a move confirmed formally on 12th May by the Bishop of Salisbury. The abbot became the rector and patron of the benefice (known as the 'impropriate' rector, a term which continued into the 19th century), although the church house, garden, and some land and local dues were reserved for the vicar. For some time the monks were housed at Newton in a building of some size. The building was later used as a school; the exact site is unknown, but its existence is certain as rent was paid for it.

John Selwood, one of Glastonbury's last abbots and a prolific builder of churches, was responsible for building the Town Bridge and, in 1486, for the rebuilding of St

> **WHO IS THE WEALTHIEST IN THE LAND?**
> The 17th-century Rector of Broadwindsor and a witty preacher, Thomas Fuller quipped that 'If the Abbot of Glastonbury could marry the Abbess of Shaftesbury their heir would hold more land than the King of England.'

Mary's Church, with its fine wagon roof.

Glastonbury held sway over Sturminster Newton for 572 years, until the dissolution of the monasteries, when the abbey was ransacked and dissolved (1539), and the last abbot, Richard Whyting, was hanged on Glastonbury Tor.

The link with Glastonbury ended, the patronage of the Sturminster living went to the Crown. Henry VIII gave it to his queen Katherine Parr, along with the manor at Newton. The living eventually passed to the local landowners, the Pitt family.

Christian practice in Sturminster does not seem to have been much perturbed by the Reformation. However, the puritanical era of the Parliamentarians under Oliver Cromwell was decidedly less calm. Vicars were imposed upon the church and St Mary's 'intruders' – Thomas Branker and John Duperier – are listed on the roll of incumbents in the south aisle. The Restoration did not result in an ejection of non-conforming clergy, as happened in a number of Dorset parishes, and the routine of earlier years returned. From 1542 to 1836 the parish formed part of the diocese of Bristol; it then reverted to Salisbury.

Little is chronicled until the rebuilding in 1825 (see below), although a singers gallery was added in 1733, music for the liturgy in the 18th century being provided by singers and musicians. Attempts to introduce an organ in 1780 were not welcomed, and scenes reminiscent of Hardy's *Under the Greenwood Tree* may well have ensued.

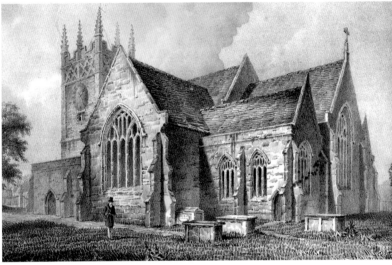

ABOVE The Revd Thomas Henry Lane Fox.

RIGHT St Mary's Church before and after Revd Lane Fox's renovations in 1825: *top* William Barnes's 1824 engraving of the church as it was rebuilt in 1486 at the behest of Abbot John Selwood; *bottom* an engraving from a sketch by W. Colbourne in 1834.

It was not until the 19th century remodelling and the arrival of a new instrument that the organ finally took over as acceptable musical accompaniment.

ST MARY'S CHURCH RENOVATION

By the early 19th century the church had fallen into a poor state of repair, but help was at hand. In 1824 the Revd Thomas Henry Lane Fox, nephew of the issueless George Pitt, second Lord Rivers, became 'impropriate rector' and curate to the resident vicar of some 24 years, the Revd James Michel. Thomas Lane Fox was to become one of the town's greatest benefactors. He took a deep interest in the parish and the education of its inhabitants. Legend has it that his kindness to local people was unbounded (and that it was often abused). In 1825 he set about making considerable renovations to St Mary's, using £40,000 of his own money and giving us the church we see today. This was a massive undertaking. Abbot Selwood's chancel and both transepts were demolished and replaced with a much larger structure. Revd Lane Fox also raised the tower from its original squat height, built the south porch, extended the aisles westwards and provided straight pews. The original construction had used weather-resistant greenstone in preference to the local Marnhull stone, but Revd Lane Fox used some Marnhull limestone to repair the greenstone arcading inside and this gives a pleasing dappled effect to the interior. In 1842 'a noble organ', built by Gray of London, was installed.

During his lifetime, Thomas Lane Fox spent nearly £100,000 on the school and the church (several million

A celebration was in order for St Mary's Church in 1986 – 500 years since Abbot Selwood's transformation of 'the Minster on the Stour'. The parish marked the quincentenary with an historical exhibition in the church hall, a flower festival, a special service of thanksgiving and 'Lift High the Cross', a pageant marking events in the religious life of the town. *Above* John Pruden, Mavis Hammond, Jill Sim and Thelma Phelps enact a scene from the English Civil War.

THE WELLINGTONIA

Towering some 112 feet over St Mary's Churchyard, the Wellingtonia tree is said to be the tallest churchyard tree in Dorset and these days is probably the highest landmark in the town. No one knows how there came to be such a splendid specimen of *sequoiadendron gigantium,* or Giant Redwood as it is more commonly known, in Sturminster, though speculation abounds: it was planted to celebrate the Great Exhibition of 1851; it was a gift from the writer Alfred Lord Tennyson; it was planted to celebrate the opening of the school or the completion of the church after its restoration by Thomas Lane Fox (d. 1861). Some memorial to St Mary's vicar and benefactor is probably the most plausible explanation (according to the Royal Horticultural Society the first seedling was not brought to this country from California until 1853). The tree, unusually, is planted 'off centre' of the main church building but its position is only a few yards from the grave of Revd Lane Fox.

St Mary's Wellingtonia measures about 28 feet in girth, nine feet in diameter and has a spread at ground level of 50 feet. At a rough estimate it would weigh about 60 tons. When Harry Dawes was teaching in Sturminster he sometimes set his mathematics class the task of calculating the height of the tree. Then, to make sure that the answer was correct, he would climb to the top and measure its height with a tape. The last reading he took was in 1960 at which time he took a measurement of about 100 feet.

pounds in today's terms). His energy and generosity are still felt nearly 200 years on but he himself died, in 1861, with barely £3 to his name. He rests beneath the east chancel wall of the church he loved and served so faithfully.

Canon Richard Lowndes was responsible for reseating the nave aisles and transepts in 1884 (his father William Loftus Lowndes had previously reseated the chancel, which is commemorated by the 1865 west window), and a year later the singers gallery was taken down. Hele & Co of Plymouth built, in 1885, the original of the organ we see today – a large, two manual and pedals. It was rebuilt in 1975 by Bishop & Sons and restored by Stephen Cooke in 2000, who added a pedal reed. The church has good acoustics and is much appreciated by visiting musicians.

We must thank Sturminster craftsman and choir master William Westcott for much of the lovely woodcarving in the church including the oak choir stalls added in 1901 and the hymn boards. During 1910 and 1911 he restored the fine 15th-century wagon roof. He and his men told of how they removed lead shot from the vicinity of the 14

projecting angels, believed to be the result of Cromwell's soldiers taking pot shots while billeted there during the Civil War. The oak eagle lectern, also carved by Westcott, was dedicated in a ceremony on 28th September 1913 to the memory of Dorset dialect poet William Barnes.

The Warrior Memorial Chapel is Sturminster's tribute to the fallen of the 20th century and their names are inscribed

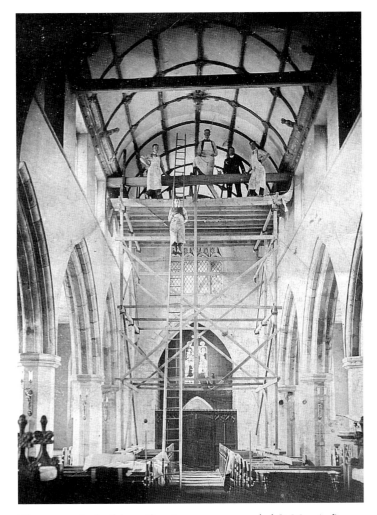

The removal of a false ceiling in 1910-11 revealed St Mary's fine 15th-century wagon roof. William Westcott oversaw the renovation: from left Harry Collins, Arthur Westcott (William's son, on ladder), Walter Roberts, Revd Hunt Gould (curate) and George Davidge. (Arthur Westcott was responsible for some of the wood carving and joinery on the *Queen Mary*.)

as a reredos. The church's kneelers, worked by local embroiderers, are particularly attractive, showing the flora and fauna of the area.

The neighbouring parishes of Hinton St Mary and Lydlinch have come into the care of St Mary's, and the vicar, assisted by lay readers and a number of retired clergy, ministers to a much wider area.

RECENT RENOVATIONS

The peal of six bells includes the tenor from 1612, inscribed 'Serve the Lord' and not recast until 1862, another of 1625, recast under Canon Lowndes, and four given by Revd Lane Fox in 1827. These bells were rehung in 1933, but by the end of the 20th century both bells and supporting frame were in need of repair. St Mary's fabric convenor Major General John Alexander put in train extensive restoration, which was carried out by Whites of Appleton, Oxon, with help in the hanging from the Army at Blandford Camp. The cost of this work, a new ringing gallery and an overhaul of the church clock came to £70,812 (the project received a Millennium Grant of £25,464). The new bells were dedicated on 14th March 1999 and rang in the 21st century.

In September 1982 the church was struck by lightning during an organ recital; local builders Hammonds were

William Westcott (centre with beard) on a St Mary's choir and bell ringers outing in the 1920s.

One of the 14 angels projecting from the side of the wagon roof, apparently used as target practice by Oliver Cromwell's men.

called in to repair a pinnacle and put up a lightning conductor.

When the former Church School was no longer needed the buildings were used as a church hall. But the structure and decoration became tired and in need of repair, so in 2004-05 the original 1817 building was restored and redecorated in accordance with its Listed Building status, again under the leadership of John Alexander. The hall has been spruced up with no loss of character, and now has a streamlined galley kitchen and a mezzanine floor that serves as a parish office. The cost of all this was £105,000, made up of proceeds from the sale of part of the building and funds raised by the community.

WINDOWS

St Mary's has some remarkable modern stained glass. The west window, depicting the Nativity, is the earliest work of the first well-known English woman stained-glass maker, Mary Lowndes (1857-1927), and commemorates her mother. In memory of her father, Canon Lowndes, she made the Resurrection Window in the south chapel. The north aisle window of 1911 is by Geoffrey Webb (his signature rebus, a cobweb, can be seen in the bottom left

St Mary's bells were rehung in 1999 by Whites of Appleton (Oxon). At Whites' factory, with the bells in the foreground and new bell wheels and frame in the background, *front from left* Phyllis Pape, Margaret Kelley, Elsie Horne, Betty Cowley, Revd John Day; *back from left* Margaret Day, an employee of Whites, Rosemary Wynn, Alan Harrison, Norah Puckett, Felicity Harrison, Major General John Alexander, Cyril Puckett.

corner), and shows the story of St Martin of Tours sharing his cloak with a beggar. It is the Art Deco south window, one of only three in England by the Dublin artist Harry Clarke, which draws the eye. Its rich jewel colours commemorate Roma, the New Zealand-born wife of local worthy Sir Drummond Spencer-Smith; she died aged only 28 in the influenza epidemic of 1918, having come over with the New Zealand troops as a Red Cross nurse. Roma is represented as St Elizabeth and, with St Barbara, flanks the Virgin and Child (a likeness based on Roma's infant son).

WORKHOUSE CHAPEL

In 1890 Montague Williams built a chapel for the inmates of the Union Workhouse (see Chapter 5) on land granted by General Augustus Lane-Fox Pitt-Rivers, on condition that it reverted to the Rivers Estate if it ceased to be a place of worship. Montague Williams died that December and his son inherited the Woolland estate, maintaining the family's interest in the Workhouse.

At a service on 3rd May 1942, the Bishop of Salisbury

ABOVE Stained-glass maker Geoffrey Webb's signature cobweb in St Mary's church.

BELOW Erecting a new flagstaff at St Mary's in 1972: Stan Score, vehicle driver, Eddie Peck, Alec Knott and Joe Fudge.

The choir of St Mary's singing carols around the Christmas tree in the Market Place in 1969. Note the old Post Office (back right) and Alex J. Hicks, now Root & Vine.

unveiled and dedicated a memorial to Montague Williams and his son Montague Scott Williams. The last service to be held there was on 27th August 1969, and in accordance with the terms agreed in 1891, ownership of the site reverted a year and a day later to the Rivers Estate, from whom it was acquired by Dorset County Council in the 1970s. The Chapel, as it had been dedicated rather than consecrated, now houses Sturminster Newton Museum.

ROMAN CATHOLICS

After the Reformation, Roman Catholics who did not embrace the Church of England were in a dangerous position. Those who refused to attend the new services were faced with heavy fines, and their names appear in documents known as the Protestation Returns. Groups of Roman Catholics, known as Recusants, tended to gather where there was some possibility of a priest saying Mass, an activity fraught with danger to both priest and worshippers. The White family at Fiddleford Mill are one example, and theirs would have been the nearest place for any Catholics in Sturminster to worship, at least until the early 18th century, when the Whites left Fiddleford. (Chidiock Titchborne married into the White family and was later implicated in the Babington Plot of 1586 to put Mary Queen of Scots on the throne. He was hanged, drawn and quartered.)

A 1680 list of Recusants names Charles White in Fiddleford and Ignatius White in Child Okeford. Also included is George Hussey of Nash Court, Marnhull, and it was from his conversion to Catholicism in the 1660s (he had married a Roman Catholic) that the substantial community in Marnhull grew – the baptismal rolls for the years 1772 to 1826 show that not only the Hussey family, but the staff and workers on his estate were Catholics. In that period, however, there are no entries for Sturminster.

In the early 19th century it was the Methodists who made great strides in the evangelisation of Sturminster Newton. Catholics came in from the cold with the Emancipation Act of 1829, and it is arguable that if there had not been such a strong Roman Catholic presence in Marnhull, a Catholic Church would have been built in Sturminster. As it was, the Marnhull congregation built its own church in 1832 (the same year in which the Methodist Church in Sturminster was built), and that is where Sturminster Catholics worship today.

NON-CONFORMITY

Dorset has a long tradition of non-conformity. A fair-sized group of Dorset men, organised by Revd John White of Dorchester, had left for North America in 1629, but by 1634 Archbishop Laud was complaining that there were 'Puritans in nearly every parish in Dorset'. However, Sturminster has had fewer examples of Non-Conformist churches than neighbouring communities such as Stalbridge and Marnhull, where, respectively, Congregationalists and Quakers both founded meeting places. (Although a number of Quakers appear under the Sturminster Division at the time of recruitment for the

The Boys Brigade outside St Mary's in 1912, led by Revd Gould (centre left wearing dog collar), curate of St Mary's and chaplain of the Union Workhouse. He went on to become vicar of Hammoon. Many of these lads would have gone to war just a few years later.

Napoleonic Wars, it is most likely that they were members of the Marnhull Society of Friends.)

CONGREGATIONALISM
Congregationalists derive from the earliest separation from the Church of England, those who, in their fervour for the Bible, wished to distance themselves further than the Puritans from the established church. The Restoration and then the 1662 Act of Uniformity led to many of them laying down their ministry rather than assent to the reintroduction of the *Book of Common Prayer*. Among these was Revd Thomas Moore of Hammoon who chose to live in poverty and obscurity rather than violate his conscience. When Charles II proclaimed an indulgence for Non-Conformists in 1672, Revd Moore was licensed to be preacher and teacher at the house of Robert Alford in Sturminster.

The only other mention of the Congregationalists in the town comes from the *Evangelical Magazine* in January

Methodism in Sturminster, produced by the Methodists of Sturminster to mark their 150th anniversary, contains this delightful poem in Dorset dialect, 'The Chapel Spider', written by Irene (née Lydford) Thomas, wife of Revd S. Theodore Thomas who was minister at Sturminster from 1949 to 1952:

We wos all brought up to be chapel,
Me brothers, me sister an' I,
An' we zat een the back seat but oone,
Ivery Zunday, cum wet or cum dry.

The zingin' wos good an' the
    preaching,
An' we listened as best as we could,
But our thoughts did get zu distracted,
By a 'beastie' – that wasn't z' good.

Ee did waait 'til the hymn before
    zermon,

An' then ee did suddenly appear,
He'd climb vrom 'is webb een the
    winder,
An' we'd watch un een trembling an'
    vear.

Down cum thic spider a-dangling,
Wi' 'is 'airy an' spindley legs,
'is body near big as a crown piece,
An' it drained all our life to the dregs.

We zat thar een vear of thic spider,
As up an' a-down ee did run,
We only yeard 'alf of the zermon,
An' were wishing we 'adn't a-come.

We couldn't change zeats 'cos of
    Auntie,
We all 'ad t' zit by 'er zide,
She weredn't afraid o' thic spider,
Noo matter 'ow 'ard ee did try.

'Ee were iver z'wold so they towld us,
An 'ee always escaped bein' caught,
The cleaners 'ad oft tried t' git un,
An' often the battle were vought.

But somehow ee jist went on livin',
An' noo doubt 'ould 'ave bin thar
    today,
If it 'adn't a-bin ver the vire,
Which burnt all the chapel away.

I 'spose 'twere the only real answer,
For 'e'd yeard many sermons afore,
An' 'e niver took any real notice,
'Til hell fire were raised at 'is door.

Perhaps 'e weren't really that wicked,
An' were doin' the best that 'e could,
Ver 'ow else would we kids 'ave kept
    quiet?
An' behaved as we jolly well should!

1802, which reports that a chapel was opened in this 'considerable manufacturing town, to much opposition from the populace, and some difficulty in procuring a licence under the suspicion of seditious designs'. This chapel seems to have been short-lived, and it is likely that Sturminster Congregationalists would have worshipped at the Marnhull chapel or in Stalbridge.

THE METHODISTS

The forebears of John and Charles Wesley were no strangers to Dorset. Their great-grandfather Bartholomew held the living of Charmouth; their grandfather John was at Winterborne Whitechurch and, after his ejection, served a number of Dissenting congregations in the area. As Methodism spread across the country, John and Charles visited many Dorset towns, though there is no record of their having come to Sturminster. The town had a bad name, 'proverbial for its superstition, immorality and opposition to the cause of God'.

Methodism was not easily accepted in North Dorset. When John Wesley visited Stalbridge in 1766 he left a vivid account of bitter resentment and violence against Methodists there. From about 1780 attempts were made to establish Methodism in Sturminster, but these were met with hostility. On one occasion worshippers were handed over to a guard of soldiers and kept prisoner for a night. On another a mob set the fire pump on a preacher in the Market Place.

Persecution continued until 1809 when preachers came from the Shaftesbury circuit. This marked the beginning of Wesleyan Methodism in the town. Initially a small room was hired for services, and then an independent minister handed over his premises to the newcomers. A local Society was formed, and by 1811 a purpose-built chapel

The interior of the Wesleyan Chapel in Church Street in 1909 (it was gutted by fire in 1958).

was opened. The dialect poet Robert Young relates that his mother 'took him to the chapel in The Row'. It is tempting to think that this was the site of the original Methodist meeting-place in the town.

The Church Street Chapel was built in 1832. At this time the Sturminster Wesleyan Society was under the Shaftesbury Circuit, but in 1866 a Sturminster Circuit was set up. The chapel we see today, with its façade of brick with stone dressings, was extended in 1869. At the same time a two-storey schoolroom was built at the rear. A report in the *Western Gazette* on 1st October 1869 describes the opening ceremony and celebrations – an abundant bazaar followed by tea for 800. Names from the occasion and the lists of Trustees over the years, contain many that are familiar today: Knott, Fish, Rose, Benjafield, Lydford, Barnett, Duffett, Corbin, Fudge and Ridout.

The early Methodist church soon divided into Wesleyan (trades people and business people) and Primitive (working people), and at the same time as the Wesleyan congregation was building up in Sturminster, the Primitive Methodists, came on the scene. The *Primitive Methodist Magazine* in March 1845 records: 'In Sturminster Newton, Ibberton, Hazelbury Bryan and Okeford Fitzpaine God has graciously crowned our labours in the salvation of many souls and the augmentation of our Societies.' Three years later the magazine reported: 'Here our preachers and members have often met with cruel treatment, while worshipping the Lord in the open air. On one occasion, an influential tradesman fired a gun over the heads of the congregation; but soon afterwards he accidentally shot himself with the same instrument, and expired.'

The Primitive Methodists' first chapel was by Town Bridge, in a building that had been the Greyhound public house in the last years of the 18th century. This had been bought in 1845 by James Moore, a baker of Hinton St Mary, and converted into a meeting house with a dwelling for the minister. The Bridge Chapel was made over to the Primitive Connexion (the central organisation) in 1847. From the earliest days the Primitive Methodists were the source of great revival among the people of Sturminster, and in the following years the Society flourished. A Sunday School was founded, and open air services were held at Butts Pond and Sturminster Common (Broad Oak). By 1870 Sunday numbers had risen to 200 and the Bridge Chapel could no longer accommodate the worshippers. So

A Gospel Hall women's meeting outing c. 1950. *Sitting on the bus from left* (?), (?), Mrs Beale, Miss Eva Cluett; *top of bus steps* Mrs McCandlish; *next down* Miss Briers and Miss Sylvia Steers; *standing from left* Averil Cross, Mrs Martha Drew, (?), Miss Painter, Mrs Dimond, Bessie Ellis, (?), (?), Gladys Jones, Mrs Strange, Mrs Elsworth with grandson, Mrs White and Rosemary, Mrs Fiander, Mrs Colburn, Mrs Longhurst and daughter (?), Mrs Peck and Rover the dog.

the building standing now on Newton Hill was thrown up quickly, followed by a schoolroom in 1876 and the minister's house in 1879. The chapel's foundation stone conceals a bottle containing the names of the trustees and a Circuit plan.

The Primitive Methodists beat the Wesleyans to the third

The Salvation Army comes to town in October 1898.

Methodist chapel in the locality by managing to obtain land (for £5) at the top of the rise to Broad Oak in 1869 from Henry Stroud, a yeoman farmer who had also helped fund the Bridge Chapel. Membership here has, naturally, always been small, but the chapel is an attractive little white building and holds a monthly Sunday afternoon service of worship.

In 1948 a Youth Club was started at the Newton Hill Chapel, offering the young people of the town a meeting place almost to the end of the 20th century. But by the late 1950s the building was in need of extensive repair, so it was decided to reunite the two Methodist Societies – Wesleyan and Primitive – with all worship in Church Street; Sunday School and Youth activities would remain at Newton Hill. The reunion took place in November 1958 and the Newton Hill Chapel organ was transferred to Church Street as a memorial to members of the church who had died during the Second World War.

Only a few months later disaster struck. The schoolroom and part of the Church Street Chapel were severely damaged by fire and the organ destroyed. Cecil Crew of the fishmonger's shop in Bridge Street first saw the flames and called the fire brigade. Within hours a repair fund was launched. Wincanton architect Mr A.B. Grayson's interior stands today – light, airy and uplifting. The schoolroom, with vestry and kitchen, was rebuilt as a single-storey building. The opening was performed on 11 July 1962 by one of the oldest members of the church, Mrs M.E. Barnett, whose family had been involved in the Society from its earliest days. A distinctive feature today is the carved 'JESUS' above the communion table.

Damp led to more work in 2003, and the opportunity was taken to update the kitchen and washroom, and make an additional small meeting room. These rooms are in constant use, both by the church and by organisations in the town. Coffee mornings, a Traidcraft stall, mother and toddler group, jigsaw library, some evening classes, meetings of other societies, all find a convenient home here.

GOSPEL HALL

The small brick building in The Row is the meeting place of the Open Brethren, an independent group that grew from the Plymouth Brethren. It was set up by Methodists seeking a more fundamentalist form of religion, and in its early years met in an upper room behind the old Post Office in the Market Place. On his retirement, the Sturminster postmaster (and jeweller) Jesse Meader, who had joined the Brethren, bought the land in The Row where the little chapel was built by 1932. A member of the Sturminster assembly recalls that after Mr Meader's death there was a risk of the hall closing 'because only Mr Perry and five elderly ladies remained'. So a Mr Cross was asked to leave the Shillingstone Gospel Hall and come to Sturminster. Preachers came weekly from Bournemouth, Weymouth, Yeovil and Salisbury and a fair attendance built up, swelled by returning missionaries. Worship continues in the chapel, but numbers have dwindled again to single figures. For the past 20 years or so the chapel has been kept neat and clean by local Methodists.

SALVATION ARMY

On 1st October 1898 'the Salvation Army opened fire' in Sturminster Newton – not literally, but in the language of the young evangelising body. This was reported in the Army's weekly journal, *War Cry*, and it seems their battery officers, Riches and Young, in a horse-drawn caravan emblazoned with texts, received a warm welcome. Over the next few years the officers (both men and women) detailed to look after the new corps variously recorded 'souls seeking pardon', 'one poor drunkard volunteered . . . soundly converted . . . and testified' and '35 at knee-drill [prayer meeting]'. In 1899 there was 'great rejoicing . . . God brought back two backsliders to the fold: one was addicted to smoking and had cigarettes in his pocket. God pardoned his past, he gave up the cigarettes and we burnt them in the barracks while our dear comrades were rejoicing that their sins were consumed.'

Salvation Army staff records show officers appointed to Sturminster from either Southampton or the Dorset Division until 1902, but nothing has yet been found for later years, nor any mention of the location of the 'barracks'. Local memory suggests the house in Lane-Fox Terrace, Penny Street, where William Barnes went to school (see Chapter 5).

MILLENNIUM TIME WALK

While organisations and individuals cast around for projects to celebrate the new millennium in 2000, it occurred to church reader Rosemary Wynn that most people were missing the essential religious significance of this milestone. With retired drama teacher Muriel Moss, she planned a project that would bring together 250 people for a Time Walk, a pageant in 12 scenes depicting significant events in the history of Christianity that had affected the country in general and Sturminster Newton in particular.

On a perfect June Saturday, traffic was diverted, rostra set up and Church plate burnished for a journey through history dramatised around the town by members of the three main churches (Anglican, Methodist and Roman Catholic), three schools (William Barnes, Yewstock and the High School), SNADS, the WI, Up in Smoke youth theatre group, members of the Hinton St Mary community and the Pageant Choir. Narrator Pip Taylor introduced scenes that included the Synod of Whitby, the Dissolution of the Monasteries and the demise of Glastonbury, the Ransacking of St Mary's during the Civil War and the arrival of Methodism.

The Time Walk concluded with music at St Mary's, an enactment of the Crucifixion and a song from the children about their aspirations for the Third Millennium. To the pealing of bells the youngsters led the community into the sunlight where the Rotary Club had readied a barbecue, the Silver Thread was offering tea and coffee and the churchyard vibrated to the sound of the Dorset Rural School of Music Swing Band.

CHURCHES TOGETHER

Today we are no longer raked by bitter recriminations. 'Churches Together' in Sturminster arrange joint services and other activities, including an Act of Witness in the Market Place on Good Friday and, with Christian Aid, there are Frugal Lunches during Lent and Advent. In 2000 the churches joined together with other organisations in the town to produce the Millennium Time Walk, a pageant of the history of Christianity in Sturminster Newton.

The approach to St Mary's from Church Lane before the new vicarage was built.

THREE

Schools and Education

APPROACHING Sturminster Newton from the north, the first building to catch the eye, set in spacious playing fields, is Sturminster Newton High School, with its brightly coloured panels of the 1960s. This is a far cry from the educational provision here of earlier years.

Little is known of education in the town before the late 18th century, but literacy in an agricultural and cottage industry area was probably not a high priority. Larger towns, such as Sherborne, Blandford and Wimborne, had long-established schools, and no doubt some families sent their children to these.

Children at the Church School in 1920 with their teachers: Miss Watts (top left), Miss Lily Cluett (top right) and Mrs Laura Clarke. *Back row from left* Kath Hussey, ? Bashford, Cicely Elkins, Marjorie Wareham, Gladys Yeatman, Marjorie Marsh, Marsha Beale, Ruth Clarke, ? Chapman; *fourth row from left* Maurice Stacey, Norcas Rose, Graham Phillips, (?), Arthur Harvey, Maurice Knott, Cecil Crew, Fred Painter, Maurice Meaden; *third row from left* Harry Duffett, Victor Harvey, Ernie Bashford, ? Wareham, Phyllis Painter, Olive Witt, Joan Adams, Donald Inkpen, ? Duffett, (?), (?); *second row from left* Betty Pope, Harry Hussey, Phyllis Rose, Charlie Newman, Joan Knott, Violet Inkpen, Jim Yeatman; *front row from left* Muriel Watts, Esmé Pope, (?), Dorothy Crew, Joyce Inkpen, Maude Elkins.

The former Boys School, a more tranquil private house in 2006, renamed Old School.

Compulsory education, from the age of five to 12, was not introduced in the UK until 1870; however, the Factory Act of 1844 required the equivalent of three days' schooling a week. The Church of England became the main provider of education in Sturminster in the early 19th century; the Methodist School was founded in the 1880s; and some small private schools were in existence throughout this period but have left little trace.

STURMINSTER SCHOOLS

The earliest known reference to education here is in connection with the collection of rent in 1579 for a school building, formerly the property of the monks at Newton. Hutchins in his *History of Dorset* mentions a 'tourist guide' that tells of 'a school there, the schoolmaster thereof is called Lowne, a Lancashire man'.

The references in the 19th century are much fuller but somewhat confusing as to who was being taught where and when. The Church of England schools are first mentioned in 1818 in response to a government select committee's request for information. The then vicar, the Revd James Michel, replied that Sturminster Newton Castle had a day school with about 111 boys. There is also reference to charity schools for 'the poorer classes', but what and where these schools were is not clear. The 1833 *Abstract of Education Returns* refers to one Infant School (commenced 1825, mixed), one Daily School (boys only) and one Sunday School (mixed) – a total of 426 children – supported partly by subscription but chiefly by the minister, one of Sturminster's great benefactors, the Revd Thomas Henry Lane Fox. In addition, there were five small Daily Schools where children received instruction at the expense of their parents. Thus almost a quarter of the town's population was receiving some kind of education at that time.

The original Church of England school, comprising two rooms, is the building that today houses St Mary's Church Hall and bears the date plaque 1817. Attached to the east side is a gabled house, probably built in 1825, for the schoolteacher. A smaller brick extension had been added to the west side by 1840. This school is frequently referred to as the Girls School and Infants School but is most likely to have been a mixed all-age school until the establishment of the Boys School.

The buttresses of the Boys School, built by the Revd Lane Fox for the education of 'Poor Boys of this Parish', rise steeply not far away in Penny Street. There is uncertainty over the building's date, though contemporary documents suggest 1835. Once opened, the boys transferred to the new Boys School while the education of girls and infants continued in the Church School. (The

Boys School is now a private house known as the Old School and still bears on its impressive gateway the school motto 'The Foundation of God Standeth Sure'.)

Barnes scholar Dr Bernard Jones, in his search to identify the school that the dialect poet William Barnes (1801-1886) attended before 1814, cites a deed drawn up between Lord Rivers and Revd Lane Fox in 1828 for land between the church and Penny Street. This suggests that the building of the Boys School was started between 1828 and 1835, so Barnes could not have been a pupil there. His school is identified as the three-storey mullioned windowed building towards the top of Penny Street, probably a dame school, which he left in about 1814.

Fellow dialect poet Robert Young, born in 1811 a decade later than Barnes, was at first refused admission to the Church School on account of his family's Methodist persuasion. His mother appealed to the Revd James Michel, who obtained a place for the lad. It is traditionally accepted that Barnes and Young attended the same school, but there is not sufficient evidence to confirm this. (Robert Young must have been one of the earliest pupils of the Church School).

It is not until 1863 (for girls and infants) and 1886 (for boys) that we learn about the state of education in Sturminster from surviving logbooks. These reveal a limited curriculum – the most basic arithmetic, reading and writing, some music and drawing, and needlework for the girls – and give a fascinating picture of the town: of pupils going to or returning from Newfoundland; an outbreak of smallpox in 1864 which closed the school for some weeks; and a sad note on 2nd June 1863, 'One of the infants died . . . suddenly.' The many reasons for poor attendance include bad weather, the Temperance Festival and a visiting circus. Harvest time would usually find children in the fields rather than the classroom. Girls would leave school early to learn gloving so as to bring in extra income for the family, but numbers were swelled by the families of the navvies building the railway. Measles, whooping cough and scarlet fever feature regularly.

Attendance at school cost a family 1d (one penny) per child per week (it doubled to 2d in 1875). But 1d was still too much for some families and they could not afford to

Maggie Rose transferred to the Council School (now William Barnes) in 1925 to become head of the combined Junior School. *Front from left* Mrs Clarke, Miss Maggie Rose, Mrs Elkins; *back from left* Miss Rolls, Miss Collins, Miss Pitt, Miss Mona Rose.

educate their children.

A rare mention of earlier times at the Boys School comes in the writing of Edwin Westcott (1862-1940) who joined it in 1868; his first day was marked by losing a tooth to the fist of one Samuel, who later became a good friend.

The first logbook entries in 1886 give an inkling of what a poor state the school was in and of its quite inadequate sanitary arrangements – 'one closet with two seats in a lean-to' for a school of some 50 to 80 boys. Nonetheless there seems to have been concern over the boys' health, for in 1910 a gymnasium was set up in a shed, with vaulting horse and parallel bars.

Few of the teachers were college trained, but that did not mean they were without qualifications. A system of pupil teacher training had been introduced combining instruction from the head teacher, personal study and an annual examination. After two or three years a final examination led to the full Certificate and full pay; those not meeting the required standard might become uncertificated or 'supplementary' teachers.

Miss Maggie Rose set out on this long path in 1899 when she became a pupil teacher at the age of 16. The final examination in Sherborne included reading aloud the leading article from either the *Times* or *Telegraph*, but the

Walter 'Daddy' Wilkins, a stickler for discipline but a good head teacher of the Wesleyan Day School.

day was enhanced for Maggie Rose by the purchase of a new Easter bonnet. In 1907 she achieved her ambition and became a fully certificated teacher. She returned to Sturminster as head teacher of the Church School in 1911 (on a mere £80 a year).

The Wesleyan Day School opened in Church Street in 1870, in the building that is now the Masonic Hall. Inside were two rooms and a gallery for the infants. There was no yard or playground and the children had to stretch their legs in the road outside. Like the Church of England schools, it catered for children to the age of 14 years. During the school's 43-year history it had four head teachers, among whom was Walter Wilkins. Master Wilkins – generally known as 'Daddy' – retired after some 30 years, a few years before the children transferred to the Council School in Bridge Street, and was considered by all to have been a 'good' head teacher. His desk still stands in the Masonic Hall.

When the Workhouse was built in 1838, a schoolroom was included in the plans and, from 1843 at least, there was a schoolmistress in post. By the 1890s some of the children there were attending the Church School.

COUNCIL SCHOOLS

With Education Acts requiring statutory attendance, and new building regulations, came the first Council School. The purpose-built Sturminster Newton New Council School opened in Bridge Street on 29th September 1913 with Mr W.P. Lumb as its head and 109 children aged from five to 14. Mr Lumb's first entry in the logbook included the following: 'Work carried on under difficulties. No

SCHOOL DAYS IN THE '30S
'I walked from Fiddleford to Sturminster every day. We had gardening, I remember we all had our own plot of land. We went to Stalbridge to do Woodwork as there were better facilities there. We also did boxing, which I enjoyed to the full. The cane was common and detentions were frequent. At 14 years after passing an exam you went to Blandford. Everyone had jobs waiting for them – the railway, baker's boy, work in local shops.'
Cyril Score in the 1980s talking of his school days in the 1930s

Maggie Rose retired in 1944 after more than 40 years of teaching in Dorset schools.

RIGHT The bathing island.
'Access to the bathing island was by a rickety old timber bridge probably some ten feet above the water. The facilities included separate women's and men's changing rooms, a diving board and steps down to the water. Having the river nearby was a great asset, and later on when we were at home in the water we made rafts from oil drums obtained from Rose's garage.' *Reg Cluett, 1996*

BELOW A Sturminster Boys School line-up of 1922: *front from left* H. Duffett, H. Roberts, C. Newman, J. Yeatman, B. Clarke, Vic Harvey, Frank Cowley; *middle from left* E. Matthews, R. Kite, Don Inkpen, J. Duffett, S. Duffett, E. Fudge, S. Goddard, A. Young; *back from left* Headmaster Mr Cleary, Arthur Harvey, Maurice Knott, Cecil Crew, Max Beale, assistant Mr R. Clarke.

Joyce Inkpen, S. Pope, Esmé Pope, P. Rose and D. Rose as
'Running Water' in 1926.

stock, no books, no schemes. Experimental timetable in
use.'

The new school ran in parallel with the church schools,
but 1925 saw a radical reorganisation and the separation
of Infants and Juniors from Seniors. Maggie Rose left the
Church School, taking her staff and all the children under
11 with her, to become head teacher of the Council School,
now the Junior School. It re-opened with 127 children, and
from the outset educational standards were high. In 1928
a letter came from the Director of Education saying that
the school had been recognised as a Model Junior. For
many years teachers from other schools would visit to
study the methods used in Sturminster.

Organised games were started, and once a week, during
the summer months the children were taken to the bathing
island – off the western end of the Recreation Ground –
and taught swimming. With so much of the river within
easy reach of the town, great importance was placed upon
these lessons.

Sturminster schools originally served only the immediate
area, but in the years since the Second World War many
primary schools in the surrounding villages have closed
and children from these areas now come into Sturminster.

During 1954 the school became the County Primary
School and in 1967 was officially renamed William Barnes
County Primary School. These days it has more than 200
children. It has its own swimming pool, and uses the
Recreation Ground for sports days. Gardening is a popular
activity, and the children grow a wide range of plants. An
active parent-teacher-friends association gives strong
support, and the school is well represented in local
community activities, including winning prizes in the
Carnival.

SECONDARY EDUCATION

The 1925 reorganisation introduced the Infant, Junior and
Senior school structure that we have today. With the
Infants and Juniors catered for by the Council (Junior)
School, the old Church School and Boys School buildings
were put into service for the over-11s. Bill Williams was
the head, and Mrs Hayes in the canteen, which features
prominently in the memories of all who were at school in
the 1960s and '70s.

Land for the new secondary school in Bath Road had
been earmarked for some years, but it was not built until
1960. In September that year Bishop Pike of Sherborne
opened the brand new County Secondary Modern School,
as it was then called. The original building, panelled in
blue, was designed to accommodate 350 pupils, but it
opened with 497 pupils, aged from 11 to 15 years. (It
became Sturminster Newton High School in 1968, and for
some years was a middle school catering for 11 to 14 year
olds after which pupils transferred to Blandford Upper
School.)

The first head, Stanley Tozer, shortly took up a post in
Blandford, and was replaced by Ian Russell, who served
until 1990. The new school retained the Church School
motto, 'The Foundation of God Standeth Sure' (2 Timothy
2:19), along with the badge, which also figured on the
school flag; the school hymn was 'Lead us, Heavenly
Father'.

The school operated on a house system (which still
remains today), named after local writers: Hardy, Barnes,
Young and Raleigh. The annual intake was about 100
since the school served a wide area around Sturminster.
Rural science was a strong feature of the curriculum and
the site included a farm with its own livestock, and in
Harry 'Henry' Dawes the school had a master with
expertise whose enthusiasm inspired his pupils.

The school expanded when the leaving age was raised to

ABOVE Sturminster Newton Junior School c. 1958, *Front from left* Richard Barter, Roger Beale, Richard Rose, Jeremy Barnett, Charlie Hammond, Roger Goddard, Mervin Eavis, David Fox, Raymond Rose, Jason Braham; *middle* Marie Loosmore, Mary Hussey, Jackie Frizzle, Keith Rose, Andrew Rogers, Paul Lambert, Margaret Hammond, Ina Eyres, Jackie Galpin; *back* Mr Gerald Pitman, Maureen Lemon, Penny Wareham, Hilary Mount, Pat Brockway, Margaret Puckett, Ann Burt, Myra Upshall, Jenny Tite, Pamela Matthiason.

BELOW High School master Harry Dawes with his wife Gracie, who was a president of the WI. Both were actively involved in the town.

16, and more classrooms were added as the years passed. The new developments were not without their problems. It was decided to use the diggers to excavate a swimming pool, but a wagtail built its nest in the area, and work had to stop until the eggs had hatched and the birds flown. The playing fields, too, brought an unexpected hazard as flints kept working through the new surface, resulting in cut knees. New classroom windows opened outwards over a path, and after a few sore heads a barrier was erected to prevent pupils from walking into them.

A special sixth form block was built in the 1990s, and a £1 million building for science laboratories along with art and textiles technology rooms opened in 2003.

The curriculum is wide and alongside more traditional disciplines includes Business Studies, Child Development, Food Technology, IT, Media Studies, Religious Education Ethics and Philosophy, Resistant Materials and Graphics and Rural Science. The school won designation from the Department of Education as a Specialist School in Computing and Mathematics from September 2006.

There are large playing fields for cricket, football, rugby and hockey, but sadly, the swimming pool, with its filtration system designed by wood and metalwork master Alan Rigg, is no more.

The High School has always offered a wide range of other activities, including a strong drama department. School magazines, under a number of titles down the years, showcase a huge range of accomplishments. It was senior pupils at the school, led by their Head of History, Pat Moody, who in 1963 were involved in the excavation of the Hinton St Mary Roman mosaic.

There have been French school exchanges, initially with L'Aigle, and then with Sturminster's twin town Montebourg, from which many friendships have grown. Each year, pupils from the fourth year are offered a couple of weeks' 'work experience' with local businesses in order to gain insight into the world of work that they will join in a few years' time.

Crucial to any growing school is its administration, and the High School was fortunate in having as it secretary from the start Connie Guttridge from the Church School. For the last three years until her retirement in 1981, she was bursar and in addition to the clerical work played a large part in the lives of the pupils.

PRIVATE EDUCATION

There is little information about Sturminster dame schools, so called because they were usually run by older women (possibly not much more than child minders) who charged a weekly fee of a few pence. But these would not have lasted long in the face of competition from more efficient establishments (an exception being the dame school at Lydlinch). Sunday Schools also played a part in general education, originally for those children unable to attend school during the week.

Sturminster does not seem to have had as many private schools as some surrounding towns and villages such as Marnhull and Stalbridge, although Miss Bell's in Overton, Church Lane, and the schools run by Robert Young's two daughters at Riverside Villa, are remembered. Maggie Rose attended Miss Bell's – nicknamed 'Ding-dong College' by the irreverent – but found its curriculum inadequate: writing in the morning, reading in the afternoon. Miss Bell herself is described in the 1891 census as a Professor of Music. The advertisement for the Young sisters' school described it as a Ladies Day and Boarding School.

SPECIAL EDUCATION

In 1962 the Primary School started a class for children with special needs. The class transferred in 1977 to the new Yewstock School in Honeymead Lane, which provides specialist teaching for the under-16s. Until 1995, the Adult Training Centre in Filbridge Rise trained those over 16 in various skills as well as in day-to-day living. This, now known as the Stourcastle Centre, moved to Stour View in January 1996, and the young men and women are often in town familiarising themselves with shopping and traffic.

FURTHER EDUCATION

In 1841 a Literary and Scientific Institution was founded in Sturminster, with a newsroom, 500-volume library and formal instruction, including lectures on 'astronomy, heat,

Children at the Infants School c. 1920.

music, drama, Anglo-Saxons, and witchcraft'. William Barnes lectured here in 1852. Subsequent *Kelly's Directories of Dorsetshire* mention a Sturminster Newton Castle Institute up until 1939 but give no address. There was a Reading Room above what is now Marsh's electrical shop and it is likely that the organisation (which seems to have existed under various names) was based here. Those who could read would take advantage of the newspapers; those who could not would have them read to them. Letters would also have been read and written for those who were not literate. This was also the venue for a reading circle (much as today's reading groups) and members would gather to read chapters of Hardy's novels.

Little else is known of cultural life in the town in the 19th century, although there were music teachers and a bookseller, Charles Rose, who doubled as the postmaster.

During the 20th century evening classes were held under the auspices of the Local Education Authority and the Workers' Educational Association. By 2005 most had been discontinued though a number of private organisations arrange courses, and bodies such as LearnDirect are active in teaching computer skills.

FOUR

Sturminster Newton at War

THE GREAT WAR

When the First World War broke out in 1914, Dorset regiments consisted of the Queen's Own Dorset Yeomanry (QODY), or 1st Dorsets and 5th Dorsets, a service battalion raised entirely from volunteers responding to the appeal by Lord Kitchener. Of the 338 men of Sturminster who enlisted, most would have served in the Dorset regiments but many were joined to other regiments when and where needed.

The graves of Sturminster's Great War dead are spread far and wide – from France to the Middle East – reflecting the major offensives of the conflict. Early in the war the Dorset regiments were sent mainly to the Eastern Fronts to fight the Turks, first to Gallipoli; survivors were posted to the Western Desert as part of the 2nd South Midland Mounted Brigade.

A famous charge and victory by the Dorset Yeomanry at Agagia on 26th February 1916 against the Turks and Senussi, was the subject of a painting by Lady Butler. The original hangs in Dorset's County Hall and a copy is held at the Museum in Sturminster. The Turks were driven out of Palestine with the aid of an irregular group of Arabs under the command of Colonel T.E. Lawrence. One Sturminster man, Sergeant Frederick Short, whose father lived in Cemetery Cottage, was in Palestine with the QODY and entered Jerusalem with Lord Allenby. Sergeant Short was mentioned in despatches three times, and on his return home would often describe how, on horseback, he killed the enemy using only a short sword.

Frank Lemon, who lived in the Market Place, would reminisce of a rather different experience on the Western Front in France and Belgium. Poisonous gas was first used by the enemy at Ypres in 1915, and Frank suffered a gas

SOLDIER SAM
Sam Rose went all over the world fighting for king and country as a professional soldier with the Dorset Regiment in the 1880s and 1890s. His soldiering took him to India and the North West Frontier ('lor did'en we 'ave a time') and Egypt ('too 'ot vur I'). On his return he married and settled down, but when the Boer War broke out Sam, a reservist, was called up straight away. By 1914 he was too old to serve and was needed on the land. Land agent and keen photographer Charlie Stride relates how he succeeded in getting Sam accepted into the Royal Hospital Chelsea. Sam was delighted at the prospect of wearing red again, but alas had not consulted his children. Someone had blabbed and 'ov course th'fat wur in th' vire'. His three daughters 'pitched in ter I at zuch a rate that I did'en know whur I wus vur a bit' and knocked the plan on the head. Sam, reluctantly, had to stay put.

ABOVE & RIGHT Troops encamped on Durrant Field in 1910.

attack at this time.

Many came back from France crippled, either physically or mentally by their experiences and some died a few years after the end of the war as a result. All homecoming survivors were issued with a certificate: 'With a hearty welcome home and our gratitude for the National Services rendered', signed on behalf of the citizens of Sturminster by Isaac Smith, chairman of the Parish Council. In April 1919, Algernon Ward, Vicar of St Mary's, started raising funds to convert the south chancel aisle into a war memorial chapel, which thereafter was called the Warrior Chapel; a chalice and paten, used in the trenches and hospitals of Flanders, were returned to the church and housed in the chapel.

The chapel records the names of the enlisted men from Sturminster and those of the 34 who died. They include Second Lieutenant John Morton Mansel-Pleydell (son of Canon John Mansel-Pleydell), whose recovered field cross also resides in the chapel. A plaque, formerly in the

Methodist Chapel, lists 39 names, the difference probably being accounted for by the addition of men who died shortly after 1918 as a result of their experience. Three of them – Fred Short, Jim Watts and Albert Rose – are buried in Sturminster Cemetery where Imperial War Graves Commission memorial stones were placed for them in 1929.

ABOVE During the First World War, women took over the men's work and kept the farms going – the Women's Land Army was formed in 1914-18 for this purpose. Here, women are haymaking alongside unenlisted men (older men and some tradesmen were exempt from service) on Mr King's fields by Town Bridge. *From left* May Hart, Lily Lydford, Joe Marsh, W. King, Mrs J. Marsh, Harry Elkins, Tom Giles, Bill King, Mrs King and Mrs D. Lydford.

LEFT Walter White, blacksmith at Hinton St Mary, made a holder for a 1914-18 mine washed up at Burton Bradstock beach.

Of those who died, 27 have known burial places, recorded by the Commonwealth War Graves Commission. Four Sturminster enlisted men are remembered on the famous 100ft high Helles Memorial on the Gallipoli peninsula, and others who enlisted at Sturminster are recorded on memorials in the surrounding villages in which they lived. Since the bodies of many men were never located because of the appalling nature of trench warfare in France and Belgium, most towns and villages named and mourned their missing men by erecting memorials.

ABOVE Horses of the Royal Horse Artillery at the town water trough (c. First World War).

LEFT A 'Medium C' First World War tank from Bovington in Durrant Field in August 1920. It was one of two, nicknamed Mutt and Jeff, that gave demonstrations and entered a tug-of-war in aid of the Sturminster Comrades of the Great War.

BELOW Troops on the platform at Sturminster Newton station during the First World War.

LEFT Violet Cross, from Hazelbury Bryan, served as a matron in a field hospital in France during the First World War. She was awarded the Croix de Guerre for her services to nursing and ambulance work at the front. This remarkable woman went back to France in 1940, was forced to surrender to the invading Germans, twice bluffed her way out of capture, escaped to England, joined the ATS and later in the war returned to France to help reunite children with their parents. In peacetime she became a Dorset magistrate and a governor of Sturminster High School.

Brigade (known as the KRRs). Non-commissioned soldiers were billeted with families in the town or in the skittle alley of the White Hart; the officers were housed at the Manor House at Hinton St Mary. During their brief stay the KRRs endeared themselves to the people of Sturminster, principally through their music. One local resident remembers the pleasure of dancing to the Geoff Love and Rodney Bashford bands of the KRRs as a young teenager. The KRRs left Stur on 4th November 1939 for Calais as support for the British Expeditionary Force. Almost none of them returned to England until the war ended as they were either captured or killed. The soldiers stationed at Hinton St Mary embroidered their names on a tablecloth (now in the town museum) before they left for Calais.

Preparations for civilian protection – issuing of gas masks, digging and erecting air raid shelters and mobilisation of civil defence – began well before the official start of war on 3rd September 1939. In the spring of 1940 a large air raid shelter was dug out at Bonslea and a big concrete one was built on what is now the car park at the top of Church Street. Not surprisingly there was some trepidation over what was in store. Ann Barton, who lived in the Malt House as a child, recalls that her mother laid in a supply of poison in case the German army sacked Sturminster (although Miss Barton only found out about this later).

THE SECOND WORLD WAR

Sturminster Newton, normally a rural and peaceful backwater, underwent dramatic changes when war broke out with Germany in September 1939. Luckily, the town escaped direct bombing by the enemy. For its residents, however, there was tremendous upheaval and disruption of daily life.

Because of its strategic location, Dorset was in the forefront of allied preparations for liberating Europe. Much of the county became a training ground for the military and a storage area for fuel and ammunition within easy reach of coastal embarkation points. From the very beginning of the war, troops were stationed in and around Sturminster.

The first regiment to arrive, in late September 1939, was a battalion of regular soldiers, the 60th King's Royal Rifle

NEW ARRIVALS

As early as August 1939, local schools and families were being prepared to receive evacuees from the major cities. A large number of girls from one school – the Mina Road Central School for Girls in Walworth, South London – arrived in September 1939.

Evacuees from Mina Road Central School for Girls, Walworth, South London, at Hinton St Mary.

The children, each armed with a gas mask, suitcase and lunch box boarded the train at Waterloo and were welcomed at Sturminster station by the Town Clerk and the Evacuee Organiser, Irene Oxley, before being taken to the Junior School. Each family housing evacuees was given 10 shillings a week by the government. Several of the girls were accommodated at Holly House on Glue Hill until billeting families could be found.

The evacuees and the KRRs arrived in Sturminster at almost the same time, swelling the town's population considerably that September. Virtually every household would have had its guests, a point not lost on the Germans – Lord Haw Haw, the pro-German propagandist, is quoted as saying at the time that there were 'as many evacuees and soldiers in Dorset as rabbits'.

Following Hitler's invasion of France and the Low Countries in May 1940, naval and pleasure craft from Dorset's coastal resorts took part in the evacuation of Dunkirk. Large numbers of troops and civilian refugees poured into the county, among whom were the 8th Northumberland Fusiliers, who arrived in Sturminster in a sorry state after losing their weapons and equipment in France. They regrouped and were renamed the 3rd Reconnaissance Regiment – the 'Reccies' – while they were in Stur.

The 'Reccies' certainly left their mark in Dorset. In February 1943 the County Surveyor wrote to Southern Command complaining that a big exercise around Sturminster, Buckland Newton and East Stour had destroyed ditches and grass verges and that the roads were covered with mud and grass for miles. After the Reccies had moved out, there were brief visits by a few other regiments, including an artillery unit of the Newfoundlanders on transit to Italy and the 98th Regiment of the Royal Field Artillery, who were filmed while on exercise on the field at Durrant by the late J.W. (Jimmy) Strange. It was also during this period that a series of RAF-manned Radar stations were erected across Dorset; the master station, number 7211 in the southern chain, was put up on Bulbarrow Hill and operated from 1942 until 1947.

The 'Reccies' in their heavy armour crossing Town Bridge in 1941.

THE YOUNGSTERS' WAR

Accommodating the evacuees disrupted the schooling of the young locals and newcomers alike, but classrooms were created in various venues around town. In June 1940 the girls from Walworth were at last housed under one roof in the buildings surrounding the Manor House at Hinton St. Mary, where they were joined by girls from the Holy Trinity Central School, Westminster. They all did their bit for Sturminster, putting on plays and concerts for the troops and the people of the town, and many of these evacuees clearly had happy memories of Sturminster. Not only did they come back for reunions in 1974 and 1984 but eight of them married local men and stayed in the area. After the last reunion the Walworth girls gave a seat to the town and planted a tree in the Railway Gardens.

As part of the 'Dig for Victory' campaign, the Rivers Estate let Sturminster Senior School have more ground for allotments at Rixon. A band of about 40 boys managed the school garden and allotment. By 1943 the boys had

An RAF march past during a 'Wings for Victory' fund raising campaign (c. 1942), after which the participants were treated to a slap-up buffet tea.

chalked up 27 cwt potatoes, 188lb beet, 164lb broad beans, 140lb carrots, 66lb onions and 40lb turnips as well as large quantities of apples and tomatoes. Nor was wild produce ignored: in September 1941 the entire Senior School (83 pupils, one headmaster and one teacher) spent an afternoon blackberrying and sent 150lb of berries to the Fruit Preservation Centre run by the Women's Institute.

Meanwhile, the girls learnt cookery. In 1943 the senior girls made 164lb of jam from apples grown in the school garden and blackberries collected from Broad Oak. They also knitted sweaters, socks and scarves for the Forces which were distributed through the Comforts Fund. Some of the boys became enthusiastic knitters, too, with the result that one year the school produced 60 garments for the troops. The school magazine for 1944 records that young Stan Score showed early promise of his craftsmanship by knitting a scarf.

The children of both Senior and Junior schools contributed to national savings campaigns; the most popular appear to have been 'Salute the Soldier' and the 'Combined Operations' weeks. After a whist drive, senior pupils voted to give their share of the proceeds to their relatives in the forces: cigarettes were sent to the smokers and Postal Orders to the non-smokers. The children were also encouraged to collect scraps of material – paper, rags, tins, bones, rubber and string – for the war effort. As one former pupil put it, 'Lady Haig told us that even a little piece of paper helps to make a bullet'.

Despite the deprivations of war, Sturminster people who were children at the time remember it as an exciting period when they would regularly be out at night watching the sky lit up by searchlights, 'dogfights' between fighter aircraft overhead and big explosions in the west. Trenches were built at the back of both the Senior and Junior schools to protect the children during air raids, and the pupils of the Junior School were, apparently, never happier than when a siren went off.

Adult civilians bore the brunt of war-time restrictions on food, clothing and petrol rationing and the blackout. Conditions were made worse by the extremely cold winters of 1939-40 and 1940-41, but spirits weren't dampened by the snow and ice. The frozen Stour became a park for skating, games and barbecues. Fortunately, home-produced food and wildlife were more readily available in the country than in the towns and it was fairly common practice to barter fresh produce for coupons. There were, apparently, two Sturminster women who helped trade surplus coupons, one had a shop a few houses from Tom Tribe's while the other made house-to-house calls.

THE WI – FROM JAM TO BOMBS

Everyone worked tremendously hard to support the war effort, and one of the most active groups locally was the Women's Institute, whose remit seemed to cover everything from jam to bomb making. Fund raising and food education were the WI's main areas of activity, but members contributed in many other ways. In the early

The drive to recruit women into the Women's Land Army (WLA) increased in 1940 after German U-boat action against merchant shipping raised fears that Britain would starve. Sturminster's 'Land Girls' were billeted in wooden huts at Manston (where the local abattoir now stands) and were usually given a month's basic training at Mr Rossiter's farm Toogoods at Marnhull.

weeks of the war they were involved in billeting evacuees and organising entertainment for the troops. Socials, dances and whist drives raised money for the Comforts Fund for enlisted Sturminster men, who initially received cigarettes but later Christmas parcels, books and knitted garments.

The Ministry of Agriculture asked the WI to co-ordinate a Fruit Preservation scheme, which led to tons of fruit being preserved and stored. Much of the preservation must have been sugar-free as the WI in Sturminster did not receive a permit for extra sugar after May 1940.

During the war the WI worked alongside the Women's Voluntary Service (WVS) as their responsibilities overlapped in some areas. The WVS was formed in

wartime to provide support for civil defence workers and the public; they ran mobile canteens and gave First Aid, shelter and comfort to the victims of air raids. 'Agricultural Pies' were made from wartime provisions to a government recipe, and from 1943 to 1945 Shaftesbury Rural District Council ran a well-organised pie distribution operation with twice-weekly deliveries to North Dorset villages using the WVS.

The WI responded to a request from the WVS in July 1941 for help in making camouflage nets and sniper suits and, later, to assist in the collection of 50,000 cotton reels needed for insulators in army signals. In February 1942, the WI's minute books record that their members had agreed to mend 36 pairs of socks a week for the troops stationed in Sturminster.

JOINING IN THE NATIONAL WAR EFFORT

Together with the whole town, the WI was involved in wartime campaigns to raise money for weapons and equipment. Considering the relatively small numbers of people living in this rural area, extraordinary amounts were raised. For example, the proceeds of a weekly penny-per-house collection, which lasted throughout the war, were forwarded by the WI to the Red Cross and amounted to an average £10 a month (equivalent to £298 today).

Sturminster helped raise money for this Supermarine Spitfire MkIIB (P8531), 'Who's A Feared?', also known as the 'Blandford Spitfire'.

In 1940 Sturminster participated enthusiastically in the Blandford and District 'Spitfire Fund', part of a national campaign. The target was £5,000. In the event, £5,021 8s 10d was raised, which paid for a Supermarine Spitfire MkIIB (serial number P8531) named 'Who's A Feared?' Postcards of the aircraft were later sold in the local towns for 6d each. Stur raised a massive £70,000 (£2,086,000 in today's terms) in 1941 during War Weapons Week, which culminated in processions through the town with military bands playing in the Market Place

The sinking of HMS *Dorsetshire*, a County C-type heavy cruiser, on Easter Sunday 1942 by the Japanese in the Indian Ocean, sparked an enormous emotional response across the county and a huge fund-raising appeal to finance a replacement. Parades of all sections of the community were gathered in the town centre where they were urged by Mrs Prideaux-Brune of Plumber Manor and Commander Studd to make a 'big effort'. Money was sent to the Admiralty, but HMS *Dorsetshire* was never replaced.

Probably less publicised was the adoption of a submarine by Sturminster Newton. HMS *L23* was actually launched in July 1919 but was still in use in 1939. She narrowly escaped being sunk by German destroyers in 1940 – an oil slick fooled the enemy into thinking that she was scuppered – only to founder in 1946 on her way to the breakers yard. HMS *L23* is mentioned on a shield presented to Sturminster Rural District Council for its fund raising efforts in 'Warships Week'. The Air Ministry in 1943 and the War Office in 1944 also presented the town with framed certificates in recognition of its achievements for 'Wings for Victory' and 'Salute the Soldier' weeks.

Additional help on the farms and dairies around Sturminster came from the labour of Italian and German prisoners of war. Communication between the prisoners and civilians was generally prohibited, and prisoners were identifiable by their brown uniforms with yellow circles. Phyllis Goddard remembers that the German POWs were very clever at making cigarette lighters, rings and other

small items from planes that had been brought down. Prisoners were still working on the farms once the war had ended, but restrictions on their behaviour must have been relaxed as some of them remained permanently in Dorset. Several of them married local girls and settled in the town. Among them is Eric Bittner whom many will know as a painter and decorator; he married Marcia Rogerson, then of Lydlinch, and is a naturalised citizen. Helmut Eckardt was not a POW in the area but settled in Sturminster in the 1950s; his talents as a photographer have given the town exceptional service down the years.

THE HOME GUARD

Most of the enlisted men from Sturminster would have been recruited into the 4th Dorsetshires, though some would have gone to specialist units and other regiments according to demand. Those not called up joined voluntary defence organisations.

One of the first civil defence operations was to build an observation post on the hill at Rixon. This was manned by

Members of the Sturminster Home Guard practising on Okeford Hill.

The Sturminster Newton Home Guard (and many familiar Stur names): *back row from left* Ptes G. Fish, C. Hunt, I.R. Hardwidge, Cpl R. Inkpen, Sergt M. Stacey, Pte J. Crew, Cpl M. Beale, Cpl H. Crew, Ptes V. Cross, J. Elkins, A.R. Score, L.G. Tippetts; *fourth row from left* Ptes A.J. Inkpen, G. Hunt, M. Foot, E. Curtis, L. Brewer, H. Cluett, A. Mullins, F. Trowbridge, J.W. Heritage, C.E. Downes, V. Lewis, T. Hunt, W. Ridout, W. Hatcher; *third row from left* Pte A. Warren, Cpl A. Knott, Ptes F. Cowley, T. Pratt, W. Clarke, P. Dennis, L/Cpl R. Beale, L/Cpl R. Hitt, L/Cpl K. Doggrell, Ptes C. Elkins, W. Elkins, H. Deverell, L/Cpl N. Rose, Pte S. Clarke; *second row from left* Pte B. Duffett, L/Cpl W.J. Senior, Cpl J. Chambers, Sergt J. Harris, Pl Sergt L.T. Inkpen, 2/Lt G.C. Sloane Stanley, Pl Cdr Lieut J. Short, Lt H.G. Hill, Pl Sergt H.M. Beale, Sergt A. Cluett, Sergt T.H. Corbin, Ptes G. Phillips, S. Gray, P. Hart; *front row from left* Ptes Jim Duffett, P. Rose, L/Cpl C.J. Score, Ptes R.H. Rose, Jack Duffett, H. Walker, H. Matthews, W.F. Selby, P.L. Goddard, P. Hillier, T. Burt, V. White, N. Short, C. Drake, T. Gray, M. Hatcher.

a volunteer Observer Corp who were responsible for reporting any suspicious aerial sightings. When in 1940 Britain expected the Germans to invade, Sturminster responded to a nationwide appeal for all men not in active service to help in their country's defence. The combined Sturminster and Hinton St Mary Home Guard stood at about 70 men; their work was part-time – no one gave up their day job – and unpaid. By late 1940 they had uniforms and were armed with real, though largely obsolete, weapons, usually Enfield P17s rifles from the USA. The Sturminster Newton Home Guard set up its HQ at Market Cross. Official rifle practice took place on a range at Okeford Fitzpaine and the men were drilled in the market yard at Sturminster. Early in the war, street and railway signs had been taken down to confuse an invading enemy, and a removable anti-tank blockade was erected by the Home Guard on the road just south of Town Bridge.

In the event of German occupation, there were plans to establish a series of underground bases from which groups of trained men with weapons and ammunition could form a guerrilla resistance movement. This elite cadre was men with local knowledge and sworn to secrecy about their operations 'on pain of death' – even today its surviving members are reluctant to 'talk'. However, it was probably generally known that Mr White, a blacksmith, and Lance Corporal Senior, a stonemason, both of Hinton St Mary, were leading members. A group of children stumbled upon one such base in Twinwood Coppice at Hinton St Mary in 1943. Other bases were reported to exist at Shroton and Child Okeford.

ENEMY ACTION
Although the citizens of Sturminster Newton for the most part escaped any direct onslaught by the enemy, the area received some fallout from the heavy bombing of Bristol and Portland. A sprinkling of incendiary bombs fell around

Manston and a 50lb bomb exploded just outside Sturminster towards Hinton St Mary. Two land mines were dropped by parachute at Lydlinch, one in the hayrick yard of New House Farm and another in fields near Cox's bridge. In the early months of the war a line of small bombs also fell across Deadmoor Common but did little damage. On one Saturday afternoon a German fighter pilot flew low over Sturminster and strafed the town. Fortunately, no one was hurt but the steward in the Comrades Hut, Bob Hatcher, a decorated survivor of the First World War, had a close shave when the leg of a chair he had just moved was blown off.

There was a series of aircraft crashes around the town in 1941, the details of which have been well researched by Bill Chorley. The first was, tragically, that of an RAF Whitley bomber which, having set off from the north of England packed with explosives to attack German battle cruisers, was mistaken for an enemy aircraft by a Hurricane pilot. The Whitley crashed a mile north of Manston church; one of the crew died, the rest survived.

A few days later (12th April), during a heavy night-time raid on Bristol, an RAF plane engaged a Heinkel 111 and brought it down behind the Post Office at Lydlinch. No one on the ground was killed (except a few cows) despite the crash leaving a huge crater by the side of the road. All the German aircrew died and were buried in Sturminster Cemetery (see Chapter 8). Two months later, on 15th June another Heinkel crashed at Fred Vining's farm at Puxey, again killing all the crew; they were also buried in Sturminster. Debris from this crash spread over a wide area and fragments still come to the surface as the land is farmed. Shortly after March 1963 the remains of all the German airmen were exhumed and reburied at the German Military Cemetery at Cannock Chase, Staffordshire.

A final tragic air crash occurred in November 1943 when a Lancaster from No. 1678 Conversion Unit exploded in mid-air over Sturminster. Most of it came down in a field behind Newton, but debris spread as far as Piddles Wood. Bert Fish had a very lucky escape when one of the wheels landed only feet from where he had been working in fields near Stalbridge Lane. Had the explosion occurred seconds earlier Sturminster would have borne the

Former Walworth evacuees presented the town with a seat in 1984. *Seated* Sylvia Rose (née Eden); *standing left to right* June Ridout (née Coombes), Irene Moore (née Burnage), Doris Marsh (née Cramp) and Olive Rose (née Overton).

brunt of the crash.

The town's final 'military invasion' was by the American troops of the 377th Anti-Aircraft Artillery Ack Ack Battalion, who arrived in December 1943 and stayed until they were sent to France as part of Operation Overlord, the Allied Invasion of occupied Europe, in June 1944. Throughout 1943 in the run-up to D-Day, allied forces were concentrated in the south of England: British and Canadian troops to the east of a line running approximately along the Dorset-Hampshire border, the Americans massed to the west.

Elwood Turner (right), who served with the American 377th 'Ack Ack' Battalion, and military dentist Captain Kantrowitz (left) outside the Prophylactic Station on Church Street. Elwood Turner, who was stationed in Sturminster for nine months during the Second World War, married local girl Heather Hatcher.

THE AMERICANS IN STUR

The Americans are remembered with affection for both their geniality and their generosity. As the troops before them, the ordinary American soldiers were billeted in private houses and in the White Hart, Swan and Bull Inns, while the officers were at the Manor House, Hinton St Mary. Many US military hospitals were set up around Dorset, intended for war casualties, but by November 1943 they had to deal with thousands of cases of malaria and other fevers experienced by American troops returning from campaigns in North Africa and Italy. Vine House in Penny Street was turned into a small isolation hospital for non-tropical infectious diseases, its stable block a temporary mortuary. After a head-on air-to-air crash near Shaftesbury, the two airmen killed were wrapped in their own parachutes and taken to the Vine House mortuary; another resident was a young soldier, aged 27, who died of diphtheria in the days before the general availability of penicillin.

In the weeks preceding D-Day, 6th June 1944, the narrow lanes of Dorset were congested with allied troops massing towards coastal embarkation points. Solid streams of vehicles, tank transporters and gun carriers crawled along the roads. When the troops eventually left, the town had difficulty readjusting to its former tranquillity: 'Things were so quiet, it was almost unbelievable.' Among unused supplies the Americans left behind were cartons of cigarettes, which set many of the local schoolboys on the path to nicotine addiction as they puffed away in a shed in Strange's yard (now Innes Court).

Two American soldiers returned after the war to marry local girls they had met during their stay. Similarly some of the original Northumberland Fusiliers came back to settle around Sturminster after the war: Ernie Wilson, Paddy Byrnes and Jack Bell. Ernie Wilson married Nora Innes from Hinton St Mary and later spent several years working for the Sturminster Post Office.

A physical reminder of the friendly invasion is the Callender-Hamilton steel bridge, alongside the ancient stone bridge on the main road between Bagber and Lydlinch, built in 1943 by Canadian engineers to carry heavy military vehicles. This 'temporary' bridge is still in operation.

A more sober commemoration of the American occupation of Dorset is the Roosevelt Memorial Park and its monument, erected inside Blandford Camp in 1945 and dedicated to the Americans who gave their lives. The Recreation Ground in Sturminster, donated by the Rivers Estate, is the town's own public War Memorial, along with the stone obelisk inside the Rec commemorating the 50th anniversary of VE Day and VJ Day.

Eleven parishioners died in action during the Second World War; their names are recorded in St Mary's. As with the First World War, the resting places of many of them reflect the theatres and nature of the conflict: Arnhem, Victor Blake and Samuel Ridout: Burma, Frederick Painter; Thailand, near the infamous Burma-Siam railway, Charley Courage; France, Cyril Goddard and Lionel Bower; and Portsmouth, Peter Radwell and Percy Byng. Michael Jupe and H.L. Cluett rest at home in Sturminster Cemetery; the Imperial War Graves Commission placed memorial stones for them in 1949. Also to be found listed in St Mary's is the single name of David Tite, who died during the Gulf War in 1991.

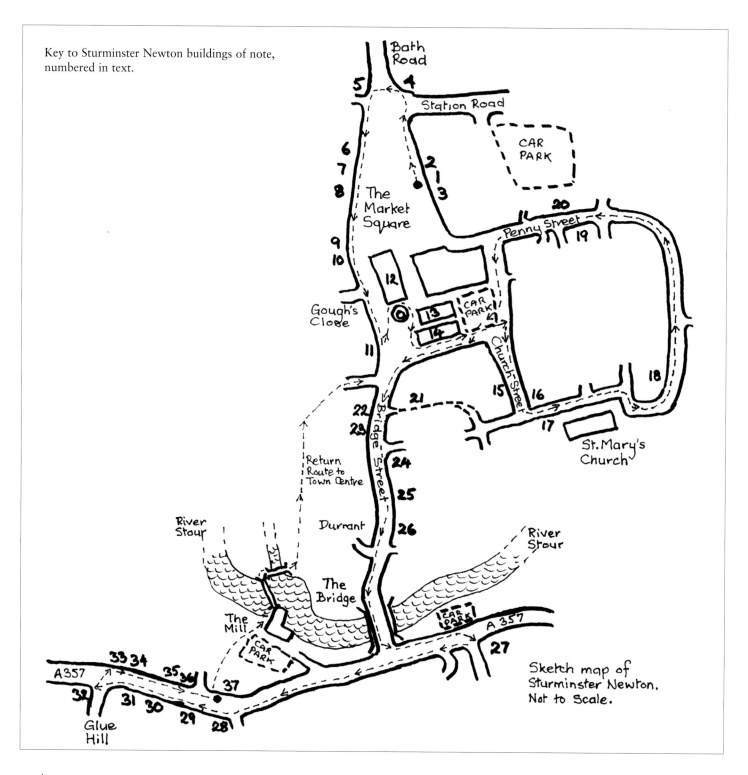

Key to Sturminster Newton buildings of note, numbered in text.

Sketch map of Sturminster Newton. Not to Scale.

FIVE

Bricks and Mortar, Rubble and Thatch

STURMINSTER NEWTON offers many architectural delights that reward close inspection – from 15th century thatch, through Georgian, to 21st century new build. Its numerous banks and public houses testify to its past as an important market town. Many buildings are centuries old, but the history of the town centre's architecture has been dictated by fire.

Stand in the Market Place and look around, not at the shops but at the buildings themselves. The newer ones are obvious: Barclays Bank, which replaced the rambling premises of Pond's the ironmonger's; and Lloyds Bank, formerly the premises of the Wilts & Dorset Bank and built originally, it is believed, on the site of the Sword in Hand public house. But most of the rest of the centre looks very much as it did when the heart of the town was rebuilt after the disastrous fire of 1729, which destroyed 67 houses, 10 barns and the Market House.

The Swan Inn (1), built in the mid-1700s, is the most eye-catching building in the square, its red brick, classical façade softened invitingly by evergreen pyracanthas. Inside, the inn has been altered, but the large fireplaces must have warmed many a traveller as his horses were changed on the journey to Gillingham, Bath or Bristol. There have, of course, been many landlords over the years. John Brown, listed in the 1823 Pigot & Co trade directory, was still the licensee at the time of the 1841 census, by then in his mid-70s. After the First World War, the landlord, W.H. Crocker, had a telephone installed – number 20, which is still part of the number today, 472208.

Down the centuries there have been other beer houses in the Market Place. The shop immediately to the left of the Swan used to be the Carpenters Arms (2). Also dating back to the mid-1700s, it may originally have been a private

The Market Place in about 1920 showing the Swan Inn with the Carpenters Arms to the left.

On the right, going out of town along Bath Road is a small, plain 19th-century stone building. Now the Museum, this was once the chapel attached to the Workhouse. The Workshouse was built as a result of the 1834 Poor Law Amendment Act and served several parishes (thus the Union Workhouse). Prior to this each parish was responsible for its own poor, and a poorhouse, funded by the townspeople, had existed behind St Mary's. The Workhouse took in the destitute of the district – people who were too poor, old or ill to support themselves; people with no family to care for them; unmarried pregnant women disowned by their families – and was funded from local rates. Thomas Hardy's description of Fanny Robin struggling to reach Casterbridge Union in *Far from the Madding Crowd* is a vivid evocation of the plight of those forced to find refuge in their district workhouse.

Workhouses were created as a more efficient and financially viable solution to poverty than paying out money in Poor Relief. They were also designed to be unpleasant for the 'able-bodied' pauper. This might have been appropriate in the industrial towns but in rural areas, where the availability of work was seasonal, agricultural labourers needed to be on hand when the work was there and needed support when there was none.

The Bath Road (White Lane as it was then) site was chosen so as to maintain a space between paupers and the 'respectable' residents of the town, and the building was erected in 1838 on the recommended Y-shaped plan. The design allowed for the segregation into two wings of men and women paupers, with sick rooms, a nursery, a lying-in ward, girls' and boys' dormitories with bunk beds, and segregated schoolrooms. High walls prevented escape and, rather grimly, two rooms were designated 'dead' and 'refractories'. The Master's accommodation and administration space were at a

The Y-shaped Union Workhouse and its Chapel (now the Museum)

central point. Alterations made in 1903 included separate accommodation for casuals, as well as stonebreaking and oakum sheds.

The Workhouse Chapel – variously described as St George's or All Saints – was built in 1890, and the last service was held in 1969 (see Chapter 2).

The number of Workhouse inmates, as they were known, varied, sometimes approaching 100. And, of course, children were born there; in 1870 boy triplets were recorded, but sadly they did not survive infancy. The local authority took over administration in 1929 and the Workhouse became the local Poor Law Institution.

In 1940 Stour View House, as it was then called, played a very different role, taking in many seriously injured soldiers who had returned from Dunkirk. Subsequently the building became an old people's home. The original Workhouse was partially demolished in the 1990s to make way for a modern day-centre for the elderly, the infirm and for those with special needs. It has well furnished and attractively decorated day rooms, a fine hall and a hydrotherapy pool.

dwelling. The pub was an ale house (it only sold beer), presided over by Miss Harriet White, the sister of a local blacksmith William White. She was a formidable woman dressed in black Victorian bodice and skirt who ruled her bar strictly, a single long room with the barrels at one end. The shop front was installed in the mid-1900s.

Beyond this building are two three-storey, red-brick shops built in the late 1800s by Mr Best, a tinsmith. His

business, located opposite, later became Pond's ironmongers, then Barclays.

To the right of the Swan was yet another licensed premises, the Crown (3), and above it the Swan Assembly Rooms. The crown-topped railings outside are all that is left of the pub today. Mr Cressey and his son had their shop here for most of the 1900s selling 'gloves, gaiters &c; sheep skin rugs, sporting goods and antique furniture,

ABOVE Charabancs gather in the Market Place (in front of what is now Marsh's) for a Parish outing in 1909.

RIGHT The corner of Station Road in 1912 and in 2006.

china, engraving &c'. Between the two sections of the building, now occupied by J. & J. Loader, is a seat where Sturminster worthies can sit and chat. This used to be the arch through which horses and carriages passed to the stables at the rear. Many important events took place in the Assembly Rooms – dinners, meetings, dances – until other, more modern halls came into being. During the First World War it became the 'Soldiers Institute', and for many years it was home to a thriving badminton club.

At the north end of the Market Place is the old Police Station (4). In the early 1800s Mr Mitchell's soap and tallow candle factory stood here. Now an estate agent's, the building dominates the view up Bath Road and still proudly announces its origin as 'COVNTY POLICE'.

At some stage in the late 19th/early 20th century certain streets were renamed. White Lane became Bath Road; the High Street became the Market Place; and the area known as Pavestones disappeared to be swallowed up by Church Street.

Sturminster House (c. 1904).

Hallett's, decked out for the Coronation in 1936 of George VI. Arthur Hallett (1865-1947) was the grandson of Sturminster dialect poet Robert Young and ran a watch making and jewellery business from this site. An unassuming man, Mr Hallett was nevertheless remarkable: he conducted a fair sized orchestra that gave concerts in the Swan Assembly Rooms; he ran a brass band; and he was choirmaster of the Methodist Church and captain of the Fire Service.

Thus on the opposite side of what was White Lane and is now Bath Road sits Sturminster House (5), once the premises of auctioneer's Senior & Godwin. Originally built in the mid-1700s, it has a typically symmetrical front and uniform sash windows giving the house an elegant frontage. The porch was added in the 19th century, but despite the alterations and its years as an office, some panelling with carved dado rails and decorated cornices remain as a reminder of more genteel times.

Opposite the Swan and between the banks sits a row of mid-18th century buildings replacing those lost in the fire. No. 3 (6), next to Barclays, had a shop front inserted in the 19th century; this became a double-fronted window sometime after 1930. It was here that, for more than 30 years, William Slade had his hairdressing rooms and also ran a tobacconist's. It was taken over by the optician's in 1992.

To the left is an attractive house (7) with sash windows on the first floor. This became a shop around 1900 and is remembered by many as Hallett's, 'watchmakers, jewellers and opticians; optical repairs and replacements; leather and electrical goods; agents for Singer Sewing machines'. Here the Town Clock (the original presented to the town by Arthur Hallett in 1921) is fixed to the wall by ornate iron brackets and tells the time for all to see.

Between this and Lloyds Bank, two adjacent buildings (8), divided by an entrance, were at one time both part of 'The Co-op'. When that business withdrew, the manager

and his assistant took over the section next to Lloyds, and for many years it was a draper's known as Sturminster Stores. The right-hand premises have not changed much in a hundred years apart from the white brickwork and two dormers. But the ashlar-veneered shop on the left is very different: its frontage is post-1918 with the doorway recessed, and three dormer windows adorn what was previously a plain roof.

Beyond Lloyds, heading south, is a row of three shops (9). The first is red brick and has a much-altered ground floor. For nearly a century the Post Office occupied the left side of the building, its sorting office and stables accessed from Goughs Close, while Jesse Meader (watch and clockmaker, jeweller, silversmith, stationer, Post Office and stamp distributor) had his shop on the right, a recessed doorway serving both. The premises next door is constructed over the cellar of an earlier building with a

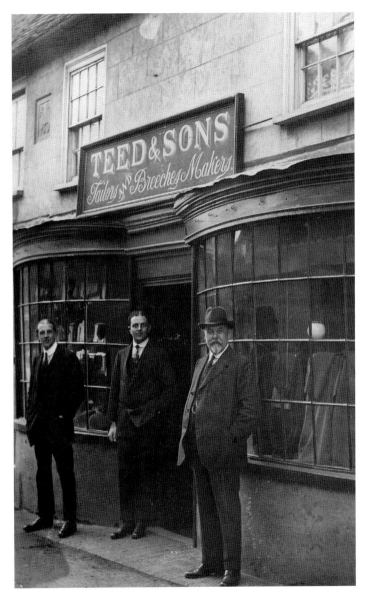

Candy's newsagent, with its fine bow windows, was once the premises of Teed the tailors. *From left* Claude Teed, his brother Ivor and their father Henry (c.1920).

solid beam supporting the ground floor that may predate the 1729 fire. Currently an estate agent's, it was for years the home of Sturminster chemists: F. Ellis in the 1890s, then C.H. Churchouse, followed by 'Scotty' Albrecht, who kept the name. In the rooms above was hairdresser Frederick Holmes, whose logo is still visible on the wall over the bay window.

The delightful 18th-century bow windows of the newsagent's (10) give onto a ground floor that has lost most of its internal walls. This building looks slightly askew: the four, first-floor windows are at different levels and there is a gap where there may have been a fifth. Not visible on the wall now, but documented, is a date-stone inscribed 'RB 1730'.

Continuing southwards across Goughs Close, three more shops dating back to the 18th century all sport bay windows to give their interiors as much light as possible; the contrasting styles lend the row a charming eccentricity.

So to the evocative White Hart (11) with its inscription 'PWM 1708', which suggests that here is the limit of the 1729 fire. With its thatch, curved door hood supported by scrolled brackets, bay windows with window seats from which to watch the town go by and archway to the stable yard, it is one of the most photographed and attractive buildings in the town.

At the far end of the Market Place, and forming an island in the traffic, is a most unusual building presently occupied by greengrocer's Root & Vine. Known as the Market House (12), it was built on the site of the old Market House that was destroyed in 1729. Its east wall

ABOVE Market Cross (c. 1948), showing the south end of Market House with the Market Cross steps, the drinking fountain and trough and, on the right, the venerable buildings marked 13 and 14 on the key. Note Cluett's sweetshop on the far right.

BELOW Tom Rose (centre) outside his butcher's shop in the Market House in about 1890 with Charlie Crew (left) and slaughterman Mr Nutt (right). It subsequently became a draper's (latterly Hicks) and is now a greengrocer's.

reveals remnants of a 17th-century stone building. The many photographs of the centre down the ages chronicle a variety of retail occupants: C.S. Hender (draper, costumier), F.G. Moore (draper, costumier), Tom Rose (family butcher) and Alex J. Hicks (outfitter's and haberdasher's). In 1958 a one-way system around the Market House was tried out; it was soon abandoned.

Just south of the Market House is the green sandstone octagonal base (c. 15th century) of the Market Cross. The shaft and cross (which may have been of an earlier date) are long gone, but the base recalls a time when the main form of official communication with the townsfolk, both religious and secular, would have been declaimed from these steps. (When he was compiling *Old Stone Crosses of Dorset* in about 1900, Alfred Pope was told by Revd Mansel-Pleydell that the old people of Sturminster said the Market Cross had been rebuilt some 100 years before, but Mr Pope could find no evidence of this.)

South of the Cross are the buildings that were beyond the reach of the great fire. Behind the Flower Shop, in the wall of the house is a small, square date-stone inscribed with the year of the 1729 fire. In this area, which is called Market Cross, is to be found one of the most unique houses in Sturminster (13). Built around 1500 as a single-

Standing at the end of White Lane Close, on the top of the ridge above the Stour, is Bonslea House. This was completed for Harry Senior, founder of auctioneers Senior & Godwin, in 1905 (as his dated monogram above the front door shows). The building is something of a curiosity because several architects were involved. Much of the roof is flat, reached by a cast-iron spiral staircase (one of the finest in the country), and the views across the river are stunning. The rainwater drains through channels into big, marble-lined tanks, which provided water for the gardens. At the centre of the now listed

house is a large hall with a decorative, glass roof and terrazzo floor (it took a maid a week to scrub it). In the winter this hall became an indoor garden of geraniums. The hall gave onto the drawing room and dining room, and the domestic area, including a spacious kitchen divided into three areas. The lower floor is built into the bank. The land belonging to the house once stretched from Denhall Close to the railway line where the family had their own halt. Bonslea House is now a family home.

Nearby is the Dower House (once The Bungalow), a charming Arts and Crafts building, much loved and carefully conserved by its present owners.

storey hall with a two-storey cross-wing at the car park end of the building, it must have been an impressive home, but it too has seen many additions and alterations. It once served as the offices of the Sturminster Rural District Council before the Council's move to purpose-built premises in Bath Road; later the Labour Exchange shared it with Mr W.H. Creech, the solicitor and Coroner for North Dorset.

Next door is Old Market Cross House (14). This attractive building, which used to house Cluett's sweetshop and restaurant (mainly catering for farmers on Market Day), still retains its 16th-century roof supported by cruck frames. Although it was renovated in 1940, some of its walls are of cob and the roof is still thatched.

Passing between these two venerable buildings, three thatched cottages stand on the far side of the car park. Much altered, but retaining their look of age, these cottages probably date back to the 16th century.

Leading south from the car park is Church Street, one of

The three 16th-century cottages on the far side of the Market Cross car park.

the prettiest in town with its parade of brightly painted doors and flower-filled window boxes. At the top are the premises of local builder Hammonds, Worton, with its elegant Georgian frontage and round fanlight above the door. Beyond, to right and left, are cottages of the late 18th

or early 19th century. In amongst these on the right is the Wesleyan School, now the Masonic Hall, and then, set back from the road, the Chapel itself. Next to it Little Thatch (15) is named for its roofing material. Like the cottages further down, it was probably built a hundred years earlier than those at the top. The Nutshell may be 17th century with an 18th-century façade, but the three cottages on and around the corner, now knocked into one

house and much altered, are even older. It is a challenge to work out where the original cottages were.

Opposite is another of Sturminster's architectural treasures, Church Farmhouse (16). Built in the early 16th century, its timber frame can be made out in the end wall. The street frontage was cased in stone in the late 1700s, probably to make it more fashionable; at the same time it was extended, suggesting the farm must have been prosperous. The interior still has a 16th-century doorway, some 17th-century panelling and original chamfered beams.

Turning left towards St Mary's Church, mullioned Stour Grange (17) is on the right. This was built as the vicarage about 1800, replacing a previous vicarage on the site. In 1923, when the Revd Harold Bowden-Smith became vicar, there were three maids and two gardeners to look after what was a considerable house along with three acres of land that included a tennis court, kitchen garden, lawns and paddock. The footpath known as Coach Road was the original drive to the vicarage.

Passing by with the Church on the right and Nazareth Lodge Nursing Home on the left, the cottage facing has retained the fine, mitre-topped iron railings, made by Sturminster blacksmith John Marsh in the early 19th century. These originally ran all round the churchyard, indeed the levelled-off remains can still be seen along the low parapet. It is thought the churchyard railings were melted down during the Great War. Those of the old cemetery were taken for scrap by the Ministry of Supply in the Second World War. Thanks to the Parish Council, the railings of Sturminster Cemetery fared better (see Chapter 8) as did the drinking fountain and water trough, which the Ministry also had its eye on.

The other side of the Church School, now the Church Hall, is the Schoolmaster's House with its diamond-paned windows, bearing the date-stone 'R S 1825'. The graveyard area beyond is the site of the original poorhouse before the Union Workhouse was built on Bath Road.

Down the steps leading from the churchyard into Ham Gate is Tanyard (18), perhaps the oldest building in the town. Its timber frame, walls of rubble and rendered cob and thatched roof suggest late 15th or early 16th century. Originally it was an open-hall house and the blackened cruck roof trusses are still visible in the roof. Sadly, the exterior now reveals little of its history.

Penny Street (formerly Tanyard Lane) has attractive cottages of various periods, from the 17th century Ham Gate Farmhouse to the 20th century houses in Lane-Fox Terrace. Approaching from the east, two buildings are of particular note. High buttressed walls rise up on the street side of the Old School (19), now a private house but built

The Schoolmaster's House, built in 1825.

by Revd Thomas Lane Fox as a boys school in about 1835; its gates of wrought iron were made in the 19th century and bear the coat of arms that is still the badge of Sturminster High School.

Dialect poet William Barnes went to work at and left an inscription on an interior wall of the second house of special interest, Vine House (20), opposite the school gates. Built in the 17th century and extended in the 18th, it graces the road with its wisteria-covered façade; the older part has mullioned windows, the right 'newer' side sash windows. Barnes' dame school was the deceptively new-looking three-storey house at No. 3 Lane-Fox Terrace. It has been suggested that this was once a printer's and a Salvation Army hall. It was also the home and workplace of John Pope, the local cooper, who kept his pony in a shed at the front. Local writer Olive Knott recorded how her father told of some Russians who brought two performing bears to town and, unable to find quarters, spent the night with their bears in Mr Pope's shed.

Down Bridge Street towards the river, the buildings nearest the Market Place and facing each other – the baker's and the Indian restaurant – are the oldest on this street, early 17th century. It is worth going up Dovers

A rare example of overhang in Dovers Entry at the top of Bridge Street. Timber beams support the jettied 16th-century first floor.

The Old Malt House, once St Mary's Nursing Home, was probably originally two houses.

Entry (21) just beside the restaurant to look at the house behind, which may be even older: it has a jettied first floor on strong timber beams, though somewhat spoiled by the corrugated-iron cladding. Next to the bakery is the Clock House (22), a mid-18th century building with delightful windows divided by narrow columns and clock over the central, recessed doorway. This was run for many years from the 1920s by Bertie Hanks, 'watch and clockmaker, jeweller, silversmith, stationer, fancy goods, toys, sports goods &c. & lending library'.

Beyond Retsel House, the new block built to replace Harding's shop after the 1956 fire, is Hill House (23), a real Jane Austen house, with sash windows under brick arches and a central door topped by a fanlight in a moulded frame.

The attractive frontage of Hanks' Clock House, also home to a lending library.

Seventeenth century Beech House.

Further down on the left is the Old Malt House (24), formerly two 18th-century thatched houses linked together in the 19th century. It became St Mary's Nursing Home between the early 1900s and the early 1930s, and several Sturminster worthies were born there. A large, vaulted cellar gives onto the road, in use when traffic was not such a danger.

Minster House (25), opposite the entrance to William Barnes School, was built early in the 17th century and is reputed to have been constructed from materials salvaged from Sturminster 'castle', although it has since been renovated and refaced.

The last major building on the Sturminster side of Town Bridge is Beech House (26). Set in grounds that give a view down to the river, this handsome 17th-century house was 'T' shaped until extended to the east in the 18th century when the three-storey porch was also added. The south-facing front has mullioned windows and dormer windows in the attic. Sadly the beech trees that lined the road boundary have had to be removed.

Town Bridge itself is one of the finest medieval bridges in Dorset. John Leland, antiquary to Henry VIII, wrote: 'There is a very fair bridge of 6 archis at the towne end, made in later times, chiefly by the vicare of Stourminstre.' The vicar referred to was probably Thomas Goldwegge, but the prime mover was John Selwood, Abbot of Glastonbury, who was also responsible for the rebuilding of St Mary's Church in 1486. The ashlar and rubble bridge was originally about 12 feet wide but, with the increase in traffic, it was widened in the 17th century and the parapet added in the 18th century. The last major work was the building of the causeway on the north side in the early 19th century, around the time of the placing of the transportation plaque and other work on the bridge in 1826. Today's heavy vehicles being no respecters of venerability, running repairs are constantly being made to the stonework. It must be assumed that there was some kind of wooden bridge as a dry river crossing before the stone bridge we see today.

Over the bridge and to the left is the Bull Inn (27). This pub was a cottage in the 17th century and, despite additions and alterations, it still feels like a house rather

A view of Town Bridge showing the slipway that gave livestock access to the water.

than an inn. To the right of the bridge and up past the Mill, is Newton, a group of remarkable houses that motorists negotiating the bends often do not have time to appreciate. First on the left is No. 82 (28), a thatched house of the 15th or early 16th century. Internally there are two jointed cruck trusses (smoke blackened in the roof) suggesting a

No. 82 Newton in 1916.

ABOVE An unusual view of Newton showing the back of No. 86 and, across the road, Newton House.

LEFT Newton House, showing the classical porch with its frieze of Wedgewood style medallions.

building of open-hall design. The Retreat, next door, is young by comparison, built in about 1800. This charming house is symmetrical but has an unusual, continuous timber lintel across the front door and windows. Next along are two adjoining thatched cottages, Nos 84 and 85, set at right-angles to each other; No. 84 has leaded lights in the upstairs windows.

Newton House (29) is dated 1789 (there is a date stone on the left chimney stack) and has been decorated in the classical style. It is the porch that catches the eye, with its flower-topped Doric columns and its frieze of Wedgwood-style medallions. Between Newton House and Barton House, No. 89 (30) looks rather severe by contrast, being of ashlar with a slate roof adorned by a wooden-latticed porch.

Although it looks magnificent and is very old, with its diamond lead-paned windows and half-timbered exterior, Barton House (31) has been extensively added to and altered in the last 100 years. Its five dormer windows at the front are all different. Hearsay has it that Tolpuddle

Martyrs sympathisers – labourers who sought to raise their wages – held secret gatherings here and were guided to the house by a lighted candle in the window.

Across the bottom of Glue Hill is Barton Farmhouse (32); its trellised porch opening directly onto the narrow pavement speaks of less busy roads. To the left is a blocked doorway, now with a small window inserted, which suggests that the building may once have been two dwellings.

On the other side of the main road is Vine Cottage, No. 93 (33), built about 1800 and connecting to No. 92, the former Red Lion public house. The brick arches over the windows and doors have distinctive keystones. Adjoining this to the left, though now removed, was Sam Harvey's original garage before he moved to premises in Bath Road (later superseded by Reddleman House). No. 92 (34), built in the early 19th century and previously the Red Lion, has been converted to a private house and the land around it developed to give the only modern houses along the main road at Newton.

ABOVE Barton House. In former times the section on the left of the house was a cattle barn.

BELOW Vine Cottage (No. 93) when it was still attached to Harvey's garage.

ABOVE A fine exposed cruck truss at No. 86.

BELOW Dangerously positioned these days, Inglenook and its warning signs.

Returning along the road towards town there are three more of Newton's gems. Inglenook (35) is the first, probably built in the 17th century of 'coursed rubble' and thatched roof; its ground-floor windows have wooden lintels and at some stage the doorways onto the roadway have been blocked. The warning triangles are a reminder of how close the walls are to the articulated lorries that thunder along the A357. In a slightly safer position is the Old Mill House (36) on the corner of Stalbridge Lane. Of similar age and construction to Inglenook, the rubble has been colour-washed, the roof tiles and the front door protected in the last century by a porch. To the rear, beside the lane, is the former stable block.

And finally, No. 86 (37), a single-storied 15th/early 16th century thatched house with later additions and facings. At the left end is an exposed jointed cruck truss filled with brick and at the east end the rendering has been removed and a similar cruck truss has been attractively exposed.

Between the wars Sturminster considerably extended its housing area. Most of this development was along the Bath Road in 1930. After the Second World War there was a great output of council housing, resulting in a whole new suburb along the rise on the Manston Road. Since then, at various stages, almost the entire Butts Pond valley – between the V-shaped arms of Bath Road and Manston Road – has been filled with new build, most recently the Honeymead Lane developments.

SIX

Literary Connections

STURMINSTER can justifiably claim association with three notable 19th-century Dorset writers whose work is characterised by a shared affection for the Dorset countryside and concern for its people. Thomas Hardy immortalised Sturminster as 'Stourcastle' in his Wessex novels. Of the three writers, Hardy had the briefest association with the town albeit the greatest reputation. William Barnes is famous in the area as a dialect poet. Lastly, dialect poet Robert Young, a friend and contemporary of Barnes, was a true native of Sturminster; while he did not achieve wide recognition, he roundly deserves to be remembered and celebrated in his home town.

ROBERT YOUNG

Robert Young (1811-1908), or 'Rabin Hill' as he is better known, was born in Sturminster, spent the greater part of his long life in the town, and is buried in Sturminster Cemetery. His mother was an ardent Methodist and when she made enquiries for the admission of her son to the Church School was famously refused. Thanks to the intervention of St Mary's vicar, young Robert was finally admitted into the Church School. He left at the age of 11 to earn his living as a tailor, but after working in various places, including London and Poole, he returned home and set up business. This proved so successful that he was able to build a house overlooking the Stour, The Hive, where he spent many happy years.

His best-known Dorset dialect poem was written in 1861 soon after the opening of the Somerset & Dorset Railway. The 169 verses of 'Rabin Hill's Visit to the Railway: What He Zeed and Done, and What He Zed About It' are full of amusing incident and humour, reflecting the poet's affection for his home town and its inhabitants, many of whom learnt it by heart and could

Robert Young aged 96 at a flower show held in Sturminster in 1907 to honour him as the town's oldest inhabitant (the chair is in the Museum).

Ah! mine is a free and a joyous life,
I bring no care, I breed no strife;
I wend my way right merrily
Till I blend with the waves in the distant sea _____

Robert Young

The Hive
Sturminster Newton

The last verse of Robert Young's non-dialect poem 'Song of Bonslea Spring', written and signed in his own hand.

recite it. His other works included 'The New Minister', 'Rabin Hill's Visit to Weston-super-Mare on the Opening of the New Pier' and 'Mapletree Farm'.

Robert Young ended his days at Riverside, a stone's throw away from The Hive and the house which Thomas Hardy had rented from him for a time. He died in 1908 at the grand age of 97.

Importantly Young left behind a record of life in Sturminster in the first half of the 19th century, an unpublished memoir of his youth written during the last years of his life entitled *Early Days*. Olive Knott and Raymond Rogers published many of these tales for the first time in 1973 in *A Pictorial History of Sturminster Newton*.

A compassionate and observant writer, Young illuminates life in Victorian Sturminster during a period of incredible change: from the farmer's wife riding to Shaftesbury market with butter in one pannier and her child in the other, to the 'swift wheels' of the bicycle and the cloud-forming breath of the 'iron-horse' (steam train). The first event he remembers is a public dinner given in 1815 to celebrate the victory over Bonaparte at Waterloo. The tables were spread in a field where from a tree hung an effigy of Napoleon. After the feast, a party armed with guns blasted away at the figure which, now well riddled with shot, was burnt on a pile of faggots. Young was later presented with the pewter plate on which one of the local women had eaten her celebratory dinner. He chronicles pranks, such as the Mitchell boys putting grains of gunpowder into the Christmas candles their father made for his customers. And he records tragedies, for example the terrible fight he witnessed in a field by Goughs Close (scene of many such encounters) between a 'corpulent young farmer and a tall wiry butcher'; the young farmer was beaten to death as his own father looked on, apparently unmoved. Throughout, Young displays a natural sympathy for his fellow human beings and, like Hardy, a sensitivity to

A POOR WOMAN'S LAMENT

(Extract from Rabin Hill's 'Sturminster Common in Zummer Time: A poor woman's lament at the labour of fetching water from Woolhouse Brook'.)

I'm tired out, a'mos' to dath!
Can hardly speak, vor want o' brath,
A-bringen up vrom Oolhouse brook,
Thease drop o' warter vor to cook.

Our Common land do stan' ser high
That pits an' ditches all be dry;
What we do zuffer none can tell!
I only wish we'd got a well.

Vor when our pit's vull up to brink,
It idden vit vor Christens' drink
'Tis all alive wi' twoads an' vrogs,
An' only good vor cows and hogs.

Our Sal went out woone darkzome night,
To vill the kittle 'vore 'twer light;
An' as we all at breakvast zot,
Whatever do 'ee think we got?

We drink'd a dish o' tay all roun',
An' then, I'll tell 'ee what we voun'?
We coudden git the warter out
Vrom our girt kittle's zmutty spout.

But hangen vrom his steamen lip
Zome slimly krissly bwones did slip.
The zight o' it took away our brath,
To think we'd bweil'd a vrog to dath.

Our Jack turned pale, took up his hat
An' went outside to "shoot the cat".
"Tiz zad" I zed "the taile you tell,
How streange you do not zink a well."

88 / LITERARY CONNECTIONS

the plight of dumb animals and creatures of the wild. The memoir now resides in the county archives in Dorchester. There is no headstone in the cemetery for this faithful son of Stur, merely an iron marker, number 674.

WILLIAM BARNES

Although William Barnes (1801-1886) is mainly remembered for his dialect poetry, he was distinguished by a remarkable range of achievements and interests – music, archaeology, physics, mathematics and social and economic reform. He was a scholar and published many books on the roots of the English language.

Barnes was born in 1801 near Bagber, one of five children (four sons and a daughter) of Grace and John Barnes, a farm labourer with a small holding called Rush-hay. William's education is a matter of some debate (see Chapter 3): he would have finished his schooling before the building of the Church School (1817) and would have been well into his own teaching career by the time the Boys School was built (sometime between 1828 and 1835), so it is most likely that he went to a dame school at the top of Penny Street. Two of his elder brothers had joined the Newfoundland cod fishing fleets, but William must have been a bright boy, for around 1814 he was taken on as a clerk by Sturminster solicitor Thomas Dashwood of Vine House and encouraged to continue his studies. Tradition has it that Mr Dashwood recognised William's talent when he saw the lad sketching in a field. William's mother and Mr Dashwood died within a year of each other, leaving Barnes bereft and unemployed. In 1818 he moved to Dorchester.

Barnes never lived in Sturminster again although some 30 years later he bought two fields here, which brought him a good deal of happiness. In Dorchester he met 13-year-old, Julia Miles, who he would eventually marry. Yet despite securing a well paid job as a solicitor's clerk, he was not happy, and in 1823 left to teach in Mere. There, at the age of 26, he set up a school at Chantry House, and hastened to marry his beloved Julia. Together they flourished: William teaching, writing, gardening and engraving, and Julia managing the school.

When hard times hit the country in the 1830s, the couple and their three children returned to Dorchester,

William Barnes.

where William opened another school, which also prospered. In the middle of his school-mastering career he decided to take holy orders, and in 1838 was accepted at St John's College, Cambridge as 'a ten year man'. He was at the height of his teaching career, but after his wife's death in 1852, his life began to fall apart and he entered a period of great grief and financial difficulty. Happily, when his school closed for want of pupils, one of his former students offered Barnes the living at Winterborne Came Church (near Dorchester). For the next 24 years he cared for his parishioners and wrote poetry, articles and books on philology, looked after by his eldest daughter, Laura. He died at the age of 85, in 1886. In these last years his poetry became popular again and attracted the attention of Hardy, who became a friend, and of other writers of the age, Tennyson, Palgrave, Gosse and Kilvert. Barnes' best known poem is 'Linden Lea', a fine example of Dorset dialect and of his love for the Dorset countryside that, set to music, has become a classic folk song. A William Barnes Society was set up in 1983.

THOMAS HARDY

For those who want chapter and verse, there are shelves of books about the great Dorset poet and novelist Thomas Hardy (1840-1928). He was not a Sturminster man, but described the two years spent here (1876 to 1878) as the happiest years of his life – 'The Sturminster Newton idyll'.

The Hardy Players in 1919.

Olive Knott.

Hardy was born at Stinsford, near Dorchester, on 2nd June 1840. His work is informed both by his love of the Dorset countryside and by the grimmer aspects of rural life. He was a keen observer of his fellows – the squire and his family, vicars and their sons, dairymaids and tranters – all of whom made rich material for his novels.

In 1876, aged 36, Hardy brought his first wife, Emma Lavinia Gifford to live at Riverside Villa, an elegant house overlooking the Stour valley. Here they stayed for two years during which Hardy wrote *The Return of the Native*. A keen gardener, he planted two Monkey Puzzle trees, one each side of the double-fronted house. This subsequently led to confusion about which side of the house he had actually lived in; the Hardy plaque was moved to the correct part of the building in 1997. The sentimental value attached to the Monkey Puzzles was such that a cone was despatched to the Hardy Museum at Dorchester, where it is safely housed.

During his stay in Sturminster, Hardy took an active interest in the life of the town, attending concerts and enjoying country fairs. At one concert the voice of a Miss Marsh from a nearby village inspired him to write some lines to her, 'The Maid of Kenton Mandeville'. He also visited Toad Fair at Bagber Bridge at which the notorious 'Doctor' John Buckland professed to be able to cure the King's Evil (a form of scrofula) by tearing the leg off a living toad and hanging it still quivering about the patient's neck in a little bag. This was supposed to 'turn his blood'.

Sturminster must have been a place of pleasant memories, for at the age of 80 Hardy made a nostalgic visit to his old home, where he apparently stood speechless at the changes that had taken place and the size of the Monkey Puzzles. He returned in June 1921 to see a performance by the Hardy Players in the castle grounds of scenes from his novels (this was in aid of the Comrades Hut Fund). During this visit he went to Sturminster Cemetery and asked the way to a circle of majestic trees nearby known as Leigh's Clump. He took tea with the Shorts who lived at Cemetery Cottage (now Acre Lodge). Their daughter-in-law, the late Mabel Ellen Penny (then married to Sergeant Frederick Short, see Chapter 4) recalled Hardy in an interview in 1966 as: 'a shortish man like my uncle Tom. He looked a schoolmasterly or scholarly type . . . He was a very quiet and unassuming man.'

Hardy died in 1928, and his heart is buried at Stinsford.

OLIVE KNOTT

Many a household in Stur will possess a copy of Olive Knott and Raymond Rogers' delightful *Pictorial History of Sturminster Newton*, one of the very few books about the town. Olive Knott was another true native. Born in Rixon Cottage, Sturminster at the end of the Boer War, she was educated at the old Wesleyan School where she was taught by Master Wilkins until he retired and the school closed down. She then went to the Council School and subsequently to Blandford Secondary School.

She decided on a career in teaching and started as an uncertificated teacher. Her first post was at Hazelbury Bryan; it was only five miles from her home but, in her own words, 'Believe it or not I was homesick.' In 1947 she applied for a teaching post in Poole, where she stayed until her retirement in 1962. Over the years she had often written poetry, and after the First World War started writing articles for newspapers and magazines, among them the *Dorset Evening Echo* and *Dorset West Magazine*. But it was not until she retired that she started writing her books about Dorset. In many of them she used the Dorset Dialect, which she loved and tried to preserve. Her work was much appreciated locally and included *Down Dorset Way*, *More About Dorset*, *Dorset Again*, *Old Dorset*, *Witches of Wessex* and, a devotee of Thomas Hardy, *Dorset with Hardy*. She died at the age of 82 in 1985.

ROGER GUTTRIDGE

Olive Knott was instrumental in the career of an aspiring young writer whose articles these days on Dorset themes will be familiar to readers of the *Blackmore Vale Magazine* and *Dorset Life*. When Roger Guttridge was 17 he chose smuggling as the subject of a local history project since a maternal ancestor was the notorious Roger Ridout, close associate of the fierce Isaac Gulliver and 'a pretty big fish locally' (see Chapter 1). The young Guttridge sought Olive Knott's advice on the project and she encouraged him. As a result he wrote two articles while still at school, one of which was accepted by Rodney Legg for publication in *Dorset, The County Magazine* (now *Dorset Life*). By now he had a taste for writing. He dropped out of Loughborough University to begin a career in journalism, first with the *Western Gazette* and later the *Bournemouth Evening Echo*. In 1990 he left to go freelance. He is a fund of information on Dorset, is particularly knowledgeable about the Newfoundland connection and smuggling, and has a long list of books to his credit, among them *Dorset Smugglers*, *Dorset Murders*, *Ten Dorset Mysteries*,

Roger Guttridge.

Blackmore Vale Camera, *The Landscapes of Dorset* and *The Villages of Dorset* (both with photographers Roger Holman and Roger Lane), *Smugglers Trails* and *Poole, a History and Celebration*. He is the son of the late Tom Guttridge and his wife Connie, who for many years was secretary and then bursar at the High School. Roger lived at Sturminster until the age of 15, then for a few years at Fiddleford. He still lives in the county.

OLIVE HALL

Another Dorset author is Olive Hall. Although not a Sturminster native, she is well known locally as her books about Fiddleford, *Where Elm Trees Grew* and *Their Own Dear Days*, are full of familiar names and references since Fiddleford is the next village downstream. Born in Poole of an old Dorset family, she won a scholarship to Poole Grammar School and went to secretarial college. She married during the Second World War while serving in the National Fire Service and worked in Poole as a secretary after demobilisation. In 1970 she and her husband Ray moved to Fiddleford. She now lives in Dorchester.

ROSEMARY ELLERBACK (A.K.A NICOLA THORNE)

There is no mistaking Wenham in *The People of This Parish*. Rosemary Ellerback 'certainly had Sturminster in mind' when she wrote this first title in the six-book saga about the three families living at Riversmead, Pelham's Oak and The Rectory, all based on real houses in Sturminster. This is not surprising since the prolific author moved to Sturminster from London in 1989 and lived in both Church Street and The Row. Writing mainly under the pseudonym Nicola Thorne, but also as Katherine Yorke, she has published more than 50 novels (gothic, historical, and contemporary), and is in the top band of most-borrowed living authors in UK libraries. She came to Sturminster by accident when a friend offered to let her a cottage; what was planned as a weekend retreat turned into a home for many years. She now lives further west.

SIR OWEN MORSHEAD

Sturminster's claim to the distinguished First World War soldier and librarian of Windsor Castle, Sir Owen Morshead, does not start until 1958 when he retired with his wife Paquita to The Lindens. He had already published several books, including *Everybody's Pepys*, an edition of Samuel Pepys' Diary, in 1926. Once in Dorset he founded and chaired the Dorset Historic Churches Trust to raise money for church repair and maintenance, and as such advised Sir Nikolaus Pevsner on his guide to the buildings of Dorset. Sir Owen completed three editions of the Trust's *Dorset Churches* and wrote a monograph on St Mary's Church, Sturminster. He died in 1977.

OTHER PENS

Many others connected with Sturminster write or have written engagingly about the area and, importantly, have contributed to keeping the dialect alive. Sturminster builder Dave England's rustic poems about his home town and county have a faithful following among local people. He was building a wall in Penny Street some 15 years ago when he was first inspired by the area's associations with William Barnes. A volume of his poems, *Days of Yore*, have been published under the Broad Oak Publications imprint. Among them is a 'Fox's Lair' a poem about local

farmer and then Town Council chairman Tom Fox, and a poem about the notorious Blandford Fly which begins (referring to his wife):

She was bitten by the Blandford Fly
I don't know why they didn't bite I.

Irene Lydford was born in Sturminster in about 1924 and educated in the town. On leaving school she went to work for the Co-operative Stores where she remained for many years. In 1952 she married the Methodist minister, Revd S. Theodore Thomas, and left Sturminster to live in Sheffield. Over the years she travelled with her husband wherever his ministry work took him, but she never forgot the beloved Dorset town of her childhood. Under the pen name 'A Dosset Maid' and writing in verse, much of it in the local dialect, she describes incidents from her early life in Sturminster. The Dosset Maid published five books of mixed prose and verse: *Zunshine een the Vale, A Bit More Zunshine, Liddle Rays of Zunshine, Zunbeams* and in 1991, *Zunshine Ave Cum*. She lives near Chesterfield.

'Marty' was the pen name of Margaret Eileen Martin who was born in Somerset in 1926 and came to live in Sturminster about 1954. A mother of seven children and grandmother to 15, she led a busy life but wrote in her few leisure moments. Her first book was *Naturewatch*, and she also wrote in verse about anything and everything she observed – wild life, old folk, children, animals.

Tim Barnes was born in the late 1920s and lived in a village near Shaftesbury. Although he never lived in Sturminster he worked for some time in one of the banks in the town. There was some talk of his being related to William Barnes whose works he quoted in *My Dorset Days* (1980), a fascinating record of life in Dorset from just before the Second World War onwards.

Some literary connections are little more than a glancing blow. In the collection *Secret Dorset*, Clive Gunnell writes of a farm near East Stour where once lived the novelist and playwright Henry Fielding (1707-54), author of *Tom Jones*. Fielding had married a Salisbury beauty of some wealth, Charlotte Craddock, and proceeded to roister and gamble away her fortune in towns such as East and West Stour, Stalbridge – and Sturminster Newton.

SEVEN

Farming, Trade and Industry

ANCIENT FOREST

In Saxon and early medieval times the lands around Sturminster Newton were part of the Forest of Blackmoor and the Forest of Gillingham. Newton was, in fact, in the Forest of Blackmoor while, north of the river, Sturminster lay in the Forest of Gillingham. These were royal forests over which the king had hunting rights, and during Norman times the forest laws were draconian. Landowners could do nothing detrimental to the king's deer. Without a licence they could not build nor could they fell trees on their own land, engage in trades such as tanning and charcoal burning, carry a bow or cross-bow; their dogs had to be lamed to prevent their use in hunting.

Blackmoor Forest, at its greatest, was 16 miles wide and stretched from Yeovil to Sturminster. King John hunted here fairly regularly (see Chapter 1) and both he and Henry II re-forested parts of the great woods. There followed a succession of de-forestations and re-forestations according to the monarch's financial needs and the pressures of population increase. By 1313, the Blackmoor Forest had ceased to exist as a forest but remained as the Blackmore Vale.

Harvesting corn the old way in the Blackmore Vale.

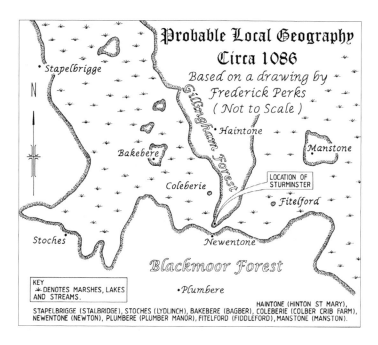

Probable Local Geography Circa 1086

Based on a drawing by Frederick Perks (Not to Scale)

Stapelbrigge

Gillingham Forest

Haintone

Bakebere

Manstone

LOCATION OF STURMINSTER

Coleberie

Fitelford

Stoches

Newentone

Blackmoor Forest

Plumbere

KEY
☀ DENOTES MARSHES, LAKES AND STREAMS.

HAINTONE (HINTON ST MARY),
STAPELBRIGGE (STALBRIDGE), STOCHES (LYDLINCH), BAKEBERE (BAGBER), COLEBERIE (COLBER CRIB FARM), NEWENTONE (NEWTON), PLUMBERE (PLUMBER MANOR), FITELFORD (FIDDLEFORD), MANSTONE (MANSTON).

FARMING

The River Stour rises at Stourhead and flows through Dorset and Hampshire for some 73 miles into the sea at Christchurch. The gradient of the river at Sturminster is very low, consequently large areas are subject to flooding. During Anglo-Saxon times the construction of numerous water mills and dams tended to stabilise the flood plains. Many of these mills, including Sturminster's (see Chapter 1), are recorded in Domesday. Over the years the valley floor has become rich pasture land, though the soil itself is mostly damp and heavy.

The prosperity of the Glastonbury Abbey was based on sheep and cattle, but this economy was in decline in the 12th century leading to the Abbey-owned land ('demesne') being let out to farm. This would probably have involved a mix of arable and stock farmed on a two-field or three-field system, each being tilled, grazed or lying fallow in turn. The land was worked by tenant farmers – villeins and bordars – who paid in kind, cash and/or labour. For example, in 1250, tenant Robert Tac paid six shillings for 40 acres. He had to work on the demesne for several days each week, and 'he ought for the whole year to carry the lord's corn with his beast as well from Niweton [Sturminster Newton] as from Burton [in the parish of Marnhull] to Glastonbury or elsewhere at the lord's will'. Glastonbury being some 20 miles away, Tac was given the consolation prize of a Christmas dinner – but he had to take his own plate to fetch it.

Frequent poor harvests, pressure on the fertility of the land and over-population led to crop failure and famine in the early 1300s. Then the Black Death struck. The bubonic plague of 1348-49 began in Dorset, probably spread from a ship berthed at Melcombe Regis. During the following decade further outbreaks occurred. The whole region was badly affected and many villages disappeared. The Black Death killed about one third of the UK population of about four million; the average death rate among tenants at 22 of Glastonbury's manors was 55 per cent. With the vastly reduced population, much of the land lay abandoned and ploughed fields were converted to grass.

Sheep farming on a large scale replaced cultivation, and

FARMING DAYS

Ken Knott was born in 1920 at Broad Oak. On his release from First World War service, Ken's father rented land from the Rivers Estate at Ralph Down, Rolls Mill.

'When I had reached the age of 12, my father would call me from my bed at 6 a.m. each morning to help him with the hand milking. I was given the easier cows to milk at first and, when a routine had been worked out, I could manage to milk four cows before I had to race back down the road and prepare myself for school. In September 1931, I started Senior School, having failed the Eleven Plus examination, mainly due to missing so much of my primary education due to my accidents and being kept at home to help on the farm in the haymaking season. I left school in 1934, hoping to get an apprenticeship with a building firm – anything other than farming, as my spirit and enthusiasm for life on the farm had been broken. My hopes were dashed however, as no vacancy could be found. Jobs were very scarce in the mid 1930s, so I was stuck with a life on the farm. Times were still hard though and I did not receive any pay. It was seven days work a week for my keep but I was allowed to catch rabbits and moles for some pocket money.'

Cider making at Hinton St Mary (c. 1900). The apples were first reduced to pulp (pomace or pummy) in the mill and pressed; the pomace was then wrapped in mats of horsehair or straw (a 'cheese') and pressed using a cider-wring. The liquid was fermented in barrels and the residue fed to pigs.

the 14th and 15th centuries saw a huge development in cloth making. Two breeds were favoured, the Wiltshire Horn Sheep and the Dorset Horn Sheep; modern Dorset Horns are still bred to this day.

The lands remained under Glastonbury until 1539. But with the monasteries dissolved, the Abbey's property was redistributed by a succession of monarchs, and in the 16th and 17th centuries most farmers in the area became tenants of the great estates. The farms themselves remained small – 30 to 40 acres being typical.

The enclosure of land had been going on quietly since about the 14th century, but the dissolution of the monasteries encouraged the process and along with it the trend towards sheep grazing, particularly in the Elizabethan period. This had dire consequences for arable and livestock farm labourers, and the expression 'Sheep eateth men' was widely used and keenly felt.

As discussed in Chapter 1, the Pitt family became substantial landowners in the area and, by a rather circuitous route in the 17th century, ended up consolidating a good deal more. The Rivers Estate inherited by Anthony Pitt-Rivers in 1970 is only a small portion of the 29,000 acres that Augustus Pitt-Rivers received in 1880, and the tenanted farms have been sold (some to their tenant farmers). But the estate still covers more than 2,000 acres and comprises a dairy farm at Hinton and various blocks of arable.

By the mid-1960s, the Blackmore Vale was still made up,

in the main, of small dairy farms, averaging around 100 acres and comprising a family unit with a full time labourer and some casual help. In 1984, the total population of Dorset was more than half a million yet only about 6,000 people were actively engaged in agricultural work. Nevertheless, agriculture still remained Dorset's chief, and highly productive, industry. Even those who weren't employed directly in farming often had a variety of seasonal jobs, for example, milking, hedge laying, shifting hay bales and general farm labouring.

Sturminster still has its own abattoir on the Manston Road, but since the closure of the livestock market in 1997 and the Milk Factory in 2000 (see below), many associated agricultural firms have either gone out of business or left the area. There are now fewer than a dozen working dairy farms in the parish.

Cows outside Market House. By the late 19th century each type of animal was allocated a different area of the town centre on Market Day: sheep by the old Senior & Godwin office in Bath Road; pigs from the Market Cross to the top of Church Street; horses and ponies from the corner of Bath Road down Station Road. Cattle and horses were also tied to posts and rails – some of which still remain – around the Market Place.

THE LIVESTOCK MARKETS

Historically, Sturminster Newton has made its reputation as a market town, its royal charters for fairs and livestock markets granted successively by Henry III, Edward I, Edward III and Henry VII (see Chapter 1). The first market site was probably to the west of the church before moving to a market place around the Market Cross and Market House. By the late 19th century the different types of animal – sheep, pigs, horses and ponies and cattle – were each allocated a separate pitch in the centre of town. From

Sturminster Newton Livestock Market: auctioning calves in the mid 1990s.

the market's earliest years there was a trade in poultry and vegetable produce (trade at this time being mainly by barter). By the 14th century some manufactured goods, such as leather, were being traded too.

In 1863, the Somerset & Dorset Railway (see Chapter 8) linked the town to a national rail network with massive benefits to the area: cheap transport of bulky goods and livestock, and fast transport of perishable goods. Special cattle trains were laid on at Sturminster on Market Day and many more gallons of milk travelled into London on a daily basis via Templecombe. Milk marketing became a major Sturminster enterprise and resulted in the opening of a creamery and cheese-making factory in 1913 (see below). The development of refrigeration, too, meant that fresh produce could be marketed to consumers in London. An egg-packing station was also part of this widening market for local produce (see below).

Britain was hit by a series of bad harvests from 1878 to 1882. As usual, corn prices fell drastically, but this time the situation was made worse by the importation of cheap corn from the USA and by the first shipments of lamb and beef from Australia and Argentina. These events were to determine the future for Sturminster's market: as wheat prices fell, more and more arable land was laid to pasture and the sale of liquid milk, for which there was a constant demand from London, took over. By the beginning of the 20th century the sale of surplus calves predominated and Sturminster market gained the reputation of being Britain's largest calf market. It had grown so big by then that in 1906 it transferred to its final purpose-built site, where it expanded to cover more than seven acres.

LEFT Farmers in the calf pens: Market Day was as much about meeting up as buying and selling.

Throughout history there have been outbreaks of cattle disease or plagues, one form of which – rinderpest (also known as distemper) – raged among cattle in Dorset in 1751. A later outbreak in 1865 was a national disaster resulting in the slaughter in some counties of 50 to 60 per cent of the cattle (rail transport undoubtedly helped to spread the disease).

A different plague has become the scourge of cattle farmers since its entry into Britain in 1839, Foot and Mouth Disease. A major local outbreak occurred in Sturminster in 1935. On April 15th two infected calves were spotted at the market, having come from Manor Farm at Shroton. The Sturminster Livestock Market was larger than usual that day and more than 2,000 animals had to be killed and their carcasses burnt. The noise of cattle, many of which had already been loaded into trucks at the station, kept people awake that night, and the next day the noise of the humane killer dominated the town. The value of the cattle lost at Sturminster Market was put at about £8,000, and the government eventually paid out more than £20,000 in compensation to farmers and livestock dealers in Dorset.

The livestock market was of huge importance to the local economy. Senior & Godwin, the market operators, employed at least 15 permanent staff and another 60 or so part-timers on Market Day, to say nothing of the peripheral cadres of accountants, insurers, hauliers and so on. Some elements of the market, however, failed to survive these years: the poultry market, for example, diminished rapidly after 1963, and from the late 1960s the sale in pigs decreased drastically too. Meanwhile other aspects of the market built up and a variety of local produce co-existed with livestock sales – everything from second-hand furniture and books to home-made jam from the Women's Institute.

When the railway line was closed in March 1966 it was sorely missed, but the market continued to flourish as the road haulage industry took over the freighting of cattle and the transportation of refrigerated goods.

Sadly, however, the market was not to see out the millennium. Two factors led to its closure in 1997 in a period of general economic decline: the arrival of Bovine Spongiform Encephalopathy (BSE) and its link with the human variant form, Creutzfeldt-Jakob disease (CJD); and the sale of the market site (see Chapter 1).

Closure of the livestock market has not led to the complete disappearance of Market Day in the town. Activity is focused again in the Market Place, which is full of stallholders every Monday, and once a month a Farmers' Market sells produce from around the region.

RIGHT 'Auctioneer Richard "Dickie" Burden held weekly auctions and monthly furniture sales in the Rivers Arms' yard. He started his business in the 1970s and worked until his death in 1991 when his son Christopher took over the business. Dickie was such a character that people would come to his sales just to hear his patter. Among the items for auction were boxes of bric-a-brac, "Miscellaneous" he called them. People used to buy these, sort through them and take back what they didn't want to the next sale. Once he had a picture of a dog to auction – a border collie, he said. "That's not a border collie," piped up a woman in the crowd. "Maybe not," replied Dickie, "but it's near the edge."'
Margaret Score, 2005

ABOVE Foot and Mouth in 1935: the cremation of the corpses in the market paddock lasted for several days and was the most horrible experience for the people of Sturminster. Sixty tons of coal were ordered for the fires, but more was needed, along with buckets of paraffin because of heavy rain. The stench of burning flesh and paraffin and the pall of smoke from the fires lived on in people's memories for years.

THATCHING

Sturminster was a predominantly thatched town before the fire of 1729. While many thatched houses survive in Newton, few remain in the centre of town.

Thatching has been a tradition that has changed little since the Middle Ages. In the past, however, thatchers were farm employees, today a master thatcher is an honoured craftsman. It typically takes three to four weeks to thatch a cottage and, depending on the building's location and pitch of the roof, the thatch will last from 20 to 25 years. Three varieties of materials have traditionally been used: water reed, wheat reed and long straw. Water reed is now mostly imported from countries such as Turkey or the Ukraine, and some local farmers specifically grow thatching straw. Spars are made from hazel or willow.

Sturminster had its own thatcher in the 1930s, Theophilus Trowbridge, but by the 1960s there was a shortage of skilled workers as many had gone to war and had not returned. The Council for Small Industries in Rural Areas, COSIRA (now defunct), started teaching young people to thatch.

Farm buildings were originally thatched, not for their appearance but because thatch was cheap. However, the cost of re-thatching barns and outhouses these days is prohibitive and many of them have been converted to non-agricultural use, such as residential, craft centres and restaurants. It is probably thanks to the new influx of people drawn to the traditional thatched cottages, many dating back to the 17th/18th century, that such buildings will remain. A few years ago, the sight of new build with thatch was rare, but recently there has been a welcome vogue for thatched homes, examples of which can be seen in the courtyard development west of Newton and in nearby Shillingstone.

ABOVE & BELOW Re-thatching the White Hart in the early 20th century and in 2006: the skills have not changed greatly down the years although the attitude to safety has.

SWANSKIN

As well as farming, a number of light industries have been carried on in Sturminster. Flemish artisans and French Huguenots settled in England in the 16th and 17th centuries, fleeing religious persecution on the Continent. It is said that the Huguenots settled in the area of Gotts Corner (off Penny Street), and they have been credited with

introducing cloth making into Sturminster. Certainly Sturminster became the manufacturing centre of a unique fabric: Swanskin, a tough, coarse, white woollen cloth, similar to felt (see also Chapter 11). Its manufacture dates back to at least 1578, when local clothier James Yonge is recorded as seeking relief from duty on cloth sold to mariners going 'beyond the seas'. A flourishing fishing industry had built up in Newfoundland and the fishermen, many of them recruited from Sturminster, favoured Swanskin for its all-weather, waterproof qualities, as did the British army and navy.

The raw wool was washed, soaked and woven into 35-yard lengths as a cottage industry and the resulting cloth taken to the fulling mill. In the mill a water wheel powered heavy oak hammers by means of a series of cams. Various liquids, including human urine, were added, together with

Sturminster Stores' closing down sale in August 1993: *from left* Joan Rawlings, Jean Clark, Phyllis King and Linda Welch. (The site is now Roy Barrett Estate Agent.)

fuller's earth. The detail was probably kept secret but the resulting cloth was eventually stretched out on upright frames in local fields where it dried. A fulling mill was established in Sturminster Newton in 1611 alongside the existing corn mill, where its stone base can still be seen supporting the brick-built north wing of the mill.

By the 18th century Sturminster was the centre of a thriving woollen industry, although it did have its ups and downs, and a number of 'burials in wool' are recorded in the Parish Registers to create a steady demand. At its height in the 1790s, the Swanskin industry was producing up to 5,000 35-yard rolls of cloth each year (approximately 15 rolls every day). The 1801 census (see Chapter 1) reveals that 283 adults were employed in the cloth industry, of whom 221 women were spinners. Yet by 1823, according to Pigot & Co's directory of that year, the industry had completely died out. Extraordinarily, not a single piece of Swanskin seems to have survived.

BUTTONS AND GLOVES

A cottage (and later workhouse) industry in hand-made buttons began in this area of Dorset in the 17th century, providing employment for thousands of women and children who produced 'High Tops' and later 'Knob' buttons, among others. Metal rings replaced fabric and bone, and button making carried on into the 18th and 19th centuries. But the advent of Ashton's button machine in 1851 wiped the industry out, causing acute distress. In Dorset, whole families were shipped to the colonies.

There was also a cottage industry, and not a hugely rewarding one, in knitted gloves in Sturminster in the 1800s. Only 7d would be paid for a pair knitted with the best wool; for ordinary wool or cotton 4d a pair could be expected. An expert knitter might manage one and a half pairs a day, but most would complete half a dozen pairs a week. Leather gloves were also made, a business continued by Dent Allcroft & Co and then, until at least 1939, by Stephen Cressey & Son.

For centuries a leather tan yard existed, facing the river near the church. Large sheds on high poles stored the oak bark and pits close by were used for soaking the skins. The refuse from the pits was dried and sold in cakes, which the poor used to keep their fires alive. With a tannery in the town it is not surprising that in 1801 there were 19 shoemakers in the area. The tanner's house, the oldest in Sturminster, still stands behind the church today and is called Tanyard.

OTHER TRADES

Clock making was a Dorset speciality for some hundred years or more, and Dorset Clocks can still be found as far away as New Zealand and Canada. Sturminster had four clockmakers in the 18th century, and in the late 19th century and early 1900s Arthur Hallett carried on a watch and clock making business that was continued by his son until his retirement in the 1950s. In 1969 Tom Tribe, an expert in long case clocks, set up business in Bridge Street (formerly the premises of cabinet maker William Westcott) where his son specialises in the restoration. In 1976 Mr Tribe and a Mr Whatmoor were instrumental in founding the Dorset Clock Society.

Of public houses and beer retailers there have been many down the years – even houses of ill-repute – as one would expect in a livestock market town. Some remain, others have changed use or disappeared. The Red Lion in Newton and the Jolly Brewer beyond Glue Hill are now private houses; the Jolly Butcher up Glue Hill, the Greyhound on Newton Hill and the Carpenters Arms, the Crown and the Sword in Hand in the Market Place are long gone; and the Rivers Arms was pulled down in 2001.

TOP LEFT Sid Courage, who lived in Stur before joining up during the First World War, enjoying a drink in the old garden of the White Hart.

ABOVE The Rivers Arms in happier days c.1900, and its demise in 2001.

LEFT Maria Rose, landlady of the Red Lion in Newton (c. 1880).

In order to encourage industry in the area and provide employment, a small industrial estate has been developed at Butts Pond accommodating a range of enterprises. A newer estate has been created at Rolls Mills on the main road out of Newton.

GONE BUT NOT FORGOTTEN
The loss of the railway and the market were undoubtedly the worst economic and social disasters to hit the town, but they were by no means the only ones.

THE MILK FACTORY
The Milk Factory – also known as the Cheese Factory, the Creamery or just simply the Factory – was one of the most respected businesses in Sturminster. It was a key component of rural life in the Blackmore Vale, Thomas Hardy's 'vale of little dairies'. Through its excellent, prize-winning cheeses, the name of Sturminster Newton travelled not just nationally but internationally.

The Milk Factory was originally set up in 1913 as 'Sturminster Newton and District Farmers' Co-Operative'

Milling and salting curd at the Milk Factory (1960).

by local farmers. The Milk Marketing Board acquired the business in 1937, at which time 145 farmers were supplying milk. After deregulation of the industry in 1994, the Milk Factory came into the ownership of Dairy Crest Ltd through its cheese making arm the J.M. Nuttal Group.

The Milk Factory was best known for its traditionally made 'Tasty' Cheddar, which took 10 to 12 months to mature. Some of the medium cheese went to the Longridge Creamery in Lancashire to be oak-smoked to produce Sturminster Smoked Cheddar. The Milk Factory built up a healthy export market, particularly in Europe, with a coloured traditional cheese coated in red wax and known as a 'Top Hat'. In the 1970s Double Gloucester, Cheddar and Caerphilly cheese left Sturminster en route for 29 different countries including Afghanistan, Nigeria, Abu Dhabi and Antigua. Japan enjoyed Sturminster cheese so much that a group visited the Milk Factory to see how it was made.

By the late 1970s milk was being received from 54 producers within a 10-mile radius of Sturminster (when the Milk Factory closed this figure had dropped to around 38, a far cry from the 145 farmers in 1937). Meanwhile, the days of the horse and cart had given way to churns and lorries, which in turn were superseded by tankers and pumps.

Despite many changes to its products and processes over the years, the Milk Factory continued to eschew mechanisation for the traditional batch system of open cheese vats and coolers, so that it could produce both

traditional and rectangular block manufacture. The method required a great deal of skill from the cheese makers and ensured high quality. Redevelopment in the early 1980s increased manufacturing capacity from 58,000 litres to 72,000 litres a day. The Milk Factory was turning out up to 600 tonnes of Double Gloucester Cheese and up to 1,900 tonnes of Traditional Cheddar and block cheese a year. Hygiene and quality control were always given top priority; constant checks were made on the milk, materials and products by skilled technicians in a well-equipped on-site laboratory. In the early 1990s, £1.5 million was invested in further expansion and modernisation, boosting handling capacity to about 105,000 litres of milk a day.

For many years, the Milk Factory operated a market stall selling its own Cheddar and Double Gloucester cheeses alongside other Dairy Crest products. The long queues at the stall every Monday Market Day were legendary, but everybody agreed that it was always worth the wait.

Sadly the Milk Factory was abruptly and prematurely closed in 2000, another proud feature of the town consigned to history. However, farmers in the area have since started making their own cheese, and of course Dorset Blue Vinney is made not far away.

THE AI CENTRE AND FREEZING UNIT

In 1944 the Milk Marketing Board set up a main centre for the artificial insemination (AI) of cattle in Sturminster Newton at Rivers' Corner. Operations started in March 1947 and within the first year membership had increased by some 500 per cent and continued to rise. With a staff of seven, the laboratory was able to process about three quarters of a million doses of bull's semen a year, for use not only in Britain but across the world.

BELOW An aerial view of the AI centre at Rivers' Corner, in its day one of the largest bull studs in southern England. The tethered bulls are just visible surrounded by faint circles of browsed grass.

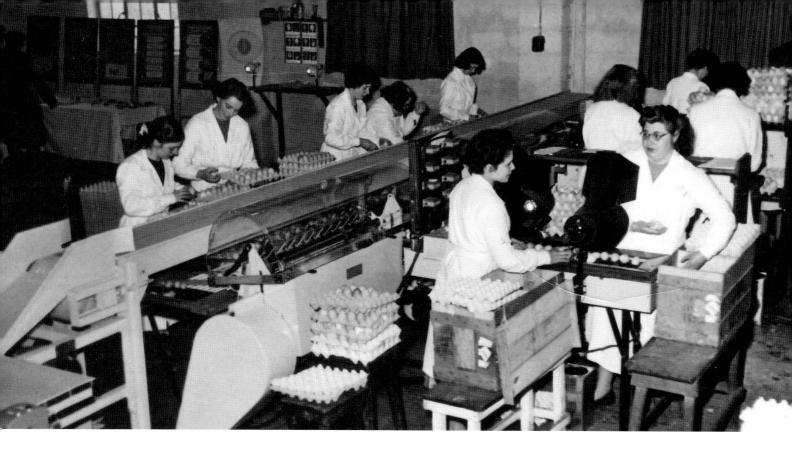

Packing eggs at the Egg Factory in 1950: *clockwise from left* Joyce Mogford, Winnie Miles, Valerie Parmittar, Stella Shaplin, Sheila Foster, Marion Short, Norma Butt, Margaret Russell, Ingrid Meder, Margaret Score, Joan Alexander.

There were around 80,000 paid inseminations carried out in Dorset and South Wiltshire in 1965. Semen was collected from the bulls once or twice weekly, frozen in ¼ cc plastic straws and stored in liquid nitrogen at -196 degrees C. At this temperature it could keep for many years. Prices varied; in 1983 for example, semen from bulls at Sturminster was sold to farmers at between £2 and £10 per dose.

A Milk Marketing Board Freezing Unit was set up in Sturminster Newton in 1966, one of only five in England and Wales responsible for the collection, processing and distribution of bull's semen for use in the AI of cattle. The unit ran a stud of around 60 bulls representing a number of dairy breeds over the years – Friesian, Ayrshire, Guernsey, Jersey, Holstein and the Dairy Shorthorn – along with beef breeds such as the Hereford, Aberdeen Angus,

Charolais, Limousin, Simmental and South Devon. Because an adult bull can produce up to 50,000 doses of semen a year, some of the bulls were very valuable and were regularly tested for the more serious cattle diseases.

The unit received visitors and trainees from home and from as far away as Zambia, Egypt, Nigeria, Kenya, India, Pakistan and South America.

Eventually the AI Centre fell victim to new methods. Bloodlines and genetic backgrounds could be studied more exactly and easily, and stainless steel vacuum flasks replaced the banks of frozen semen and embryos, giving farmers quick and safer access to more attractive bloodlines.

In 1994 the bulls left the centre, followed in 1996 by the technicians. The laboratory at Filbridge Rise, Rixon, closed in 1999 bringing to an end another chapter in the town's history. In part recognition of the centre's contribution to modern cattle breeding, the Sturminster Newton Coat of Arms incorporated bulls' heads into the badge surround.

EGG PACKING STATION

The Egg Factory, as it was known locally, was set up in the early 1900s in a wooden building between William Barnes School and Bridge Street. The operation collected eggs from outlying villages (from Sturminster to Dorchester and Sherborne), graded and distributed them. Today there is nothing left of it but a grassy bank, part of the school car park.

Dorset Egg Producers ran the business in the late 1930s, under the umbrella of National Mark Eggs. The proprietor in those days was Frederick Rowland who lived in Wee Hame, the house below the factory. By 1950 the company was owned by the Co-operative Wholesale Society, managed by Leo Plumley. The store, factory and loading bay were rebuilt after a fire destroyed the original structure, and the business prospered. Inside the factory, three grading machines were each operated by four girls. Two of them were 'candlers' – they used a light to check the eggs for any impurities.

The official definition of a 'First Quality Egg' was: 'Fresh eggs, free from taint, shell clean, sound and of good texture and shape, contents free from blemish. Yolk central, translucent or faintly but not clearly outlined. White translucent. Air space not exceeding ¼" in depth.' But many things could affect the quality of the eggs. For instance, in 1948 there was a widespread problem with certain herbs – shepherd's purse, penny cress and mathon

ABOVE Crew's, the fishmonger in Bridge Street, stocked up for Christmas 1953.

BELOW Prospect House in Bridge Street, home of basket and chair maker Henry George Bracher (centre). He pulled his raw materials from the withy bed near Town Bridge.

MARGARET SCORE'S APPLE CAKE

½ lb	chopped apple	*Crunchy spiced topping*
8 oz	self-raising flour	2 oz butter
4 oz	margarine	2 oz Demerara sugar
4 oz	Demerara sugar	Pinch mixed spice
2 medium eggs		
½ tsp	mixed spice	

Method
Rub fat into flour. Add sugar and stir in eggs. Add chopped apple. Pile into tin and cook at Gas 6 (200°C) for 30 minutes. Meanwhile, cream butter, sugar and spice together. While cake is warm (not hot) spread over the top and leave to cool.

OPPOSITE PAGE TOP Jim Boulton, driver of Strange's delivery van, outside the shop (now One Stop) in 1948. Jimmy Strange was a keen amateur film-maker and on a Saturday night would sometimes project films from his shop onto the wall opposite to entertain the townspeople.

OPPOSITE PAGE BOTTOM *From left* Jenny Douch, Iris Clarke, Dot Martin, Barbara Douch and Bet Hancock outside Stur's first self-service store, Mount's VG Foodmarket (now the Flower House), in the late 1960s.

RIGHT Amy Courage in 1937 with (not so) wild life.

– which, if eaten by the chickens, would discolour the yolks. Similarly, ducks had to be kept away from fallen acorns and willow tree roots.

The Co-op bakery in Child Okeford would use the broken eggs in cake making. The AI Centre would put them to another, more unusual use: bull's semen would be stored in whisked broken eggs which acted as a food source for the semen.

After the egg packing station closed down in 1972 two other companies, in turn, ran their business from these premises: Tutor Fire Precaution Equipment and then Rentokill. The building was finally pulled down in the 1990s.

WILDLIFE

Thanks to the Stour's fertile flood plain and its surrounding pastures and woodland, the area around Sturminster has an abundance of wildlife. Down by the Mill, one might catch the flash of a kingfisher. More common are coot, moorhen, mallard, grey heron and, at dusk, Daubenton's bat; snipe, redshank and curlew visit on migration; seed-eating siskins and redpoll can be seen in winter months; grey wagtails nest in the Mill and pied wagtails upstream in the old railway bridge. Up above buzzards wheel and kestrels scour the ground for prey. In the water, depending on the season, there is arrowhead, yellow water lily and reed, at its edge yellow flag iris, marsh marigold, tansy and purple loosestrife. On the riverbank are willow, alder and the rarer black poplar.

The Stour offers good fishing: trout, grayling, dace and chub in slower water. Otters have returned in recent years, although a sighting is very rare; walkers are more likely to hear the distinctive 'plop' of a water vole escaping into the water. In summer, dragonflies, several species of damsel and butterflies, reed and sedge warblers can be seen. Badger setts, foxes' dens and rabbit holes abound in the banks and hedgerows all around Sturminster.

To the south and overlooking the town and the valley is

Piddles Wood part of which is a nature reserve leased by Dorset Wildlife Trust from the Rivers Estate. A Site of Special Scientific Interest, it is a fine example of ancient semi-natural woodland, divided into sections of mixed planting – conifer, deciduous trees and coppiced hazel. The wood is home to goldcrest, woodcock, woodpeckers, jays and buzzards, various butterflies, fallow and roe deer, dormice, the occasional lizard and 100 different types of fungi.

Not far from Piddles Wood, in Broad Oak, is the Community Orchard, gifted to Dorset Wildlife Trust in 1979 by Ada Smee. Here volunteers manage half an acre of fruit trees, wildflowers and rich grassland. Among its ancient fruit trees are an Autumn Pearmain (variety c. 1500s), a Bramley Seedling cooking apple (1809) and an Orleans Reinette desert apple (1776).

In recent years a nature reserve has been created at Butts Pond Meadows, where thanks to the efforts of local campaigners a small pond and watercourses are home to important colonies of all three native species of newt, including the protected Great Crested Newt.

THE ELMS

Magnificent, soaring trees are a feature of older photographs of the countryside around Sturminster – elms. In the 1920s, Rolls Mill was an unspoiled paradise, the narrow winding road isolating the hamlet from Newton. There were scores of elm trees in its hedgerows, where the rooks built their nests by the dozen each spring. Ralph Down had an avenue of about 60 to 70 elms, lining the road from Road Lane Farm to Puxey Lane. These splendid trees were classified as unsafe and were felled. Since then other handsome stands of elms have gradually succumbed to Dutch Elm disease and are now only a memory.

MISS FUDGE'S SHOP

Until recently the rotted remains of a little wooden structure nestled in the undergrowth near the top of Glue Hill. This was once Miss Rose Fudge's shop. If she wasn't there, customers would knock on her door opposite and she would come over in her white apron. Newton resident, Mary Fish, remembers it well, though as she was then only five she mainly recalls the sweets: 'Rings in fondant boxes, horse shoes, liquorice in sherbet, toffee on a stick, liquorice laces . . .'. In fact, Miss Fudge sold most essentials: cards, shoe laces, cocoa, butter, sugar, tea and so on. As a child Mary Fish was much taken, too, with the shop itself: 'It was all lovely varnish inside with a counter to the right with a piece of beading along it . . . It always seemed big inside but we couldn't really have had any room. To the left was another small place joined on where Mrs Bennett used to come down the road and do her washing in a copper.' Many older residents will remember the store with affection, but it is difficult these days to picture business being carried out on such a narrow road.

EIGHT

At Your Service

STURMINSTER NEWTON comes under three tiers of local government: the Parish (now Town) Council, North Dorset District Council and Dorset County Council. The Parish Council came into being after the Local Government Act of 1894 separated the secular and ecclesiastical elements of parish government. It first met in 1896, and in 1988 adopted the style of 'Town Council'. While this did not extend its powers, it confirmed local usage and the status of Sturminster as the centre serving the surrounding Blackmore Vale parishes. The chairman did not take the title of mayor, although Cllr Tom Fox had use of the badge of office of chairman of the pre-1974 Sturminster Rural District Council (the precursor of the North Dorset District Council).

The Town Council supports community action and leads efforts to have key decisions influenced by local people and their needs. It is consulted on planning applications, and has input into highway improvements, traffic management and transport. Among its responsibilities are the Cemetery and Chapel, footway lighting in Broad Oak and the allotments at Filbridge Rise. It promotes tourism in the area and gives grants to local clubs and societies. It is responsible for parks and open spaces, and thus for the Railway Gardens, the Recreation Ground, as well as play areas at Rixon, Coles Close and on the newer developments at Honeymead and Northfields. The council was the only one in Dorset to take advantage of the 1996 Dorset Local Council Charter which allowed parishes to bid for certain principal council works – in this case grounds maintenance. It uses the 'profit' to benefit local facilities such as seats and play areas. One example is the play area created in 2005 on the old tennis courts in the Rec.

The town was never a borough, nor did it have an urban

Tom Fox (1997), Dorset farmer, town councillor and several times chairman of the Town Council.

district council. However the loss of the Rural District Council is still lamented by local people. The RDC was responsible for public health, and at various times services such as the local Ambulance and Fire services. It also had one of the best housing records in the country, for which Council Clerk (1934 to 1960) James Steptoe and housing manager Marion Bradley deserve much credit. The scheme at Bonslea Mead (see Chapter 5) was the UK's first council-built, rural, warden-assisted housing provision for the elderly. The RDC also built rented accommodation in villages for farm workers.

Since 1974, the area has been part of North Dorset District Council along with parishes from the Shaftesbury and Blandford Districts. The NDDC housing stock was transferred after a narrow vote in favour by tenants, to Signpost Housing Group in 1994, at a value of £24 million.

Sturminster still acts as a centre for caring services in the heart of the Blackmore Vale, largely run by Dorset County

Sturminster Rural District Council clerk James Steptoe and housing manager Marion Bradley (c. 1960).

Council. Examples are the Stourcastle Day Centre, Adult Learning and Family centres in the £3.5 million complex built around the former Workhouse in Bath Road, and the area offices for Social Services, housed in the adjacent former RDC and Magistrates Court building. DCC is also responsible for state education in the area and for highways.

POLITICS

Politically, the area has traditionally been a battleground between the Conservatives and Liberal traditions, the latter drawing upon the non-conformist heritage. County and District councils have been 'party politicised' since the 1970s with periods of representation by both colours. The 'Independents' ran NDDC until 1995. The parliamentary constituency, Dorset North, is now classed as a marginal seat, although the area has predominantly returned Tories to Westminster in recent years.

Reg Cluett, whose father Walter Cluett ran the sweetshop and restaurant at Market Cross, has an intriguing recollection of Sir Oswald Mosley and his Blackshirts coming to town in the 1930s, 'presumably at the invitation of Pitt-Rivers'. 'Some of the Blackshirts came into the restaurant for a meal but they were perfectly well behaved despite their origins – many of them came from the East End of London where there had been a number of riots. The meeting was well attended but I doubt whether any of the locals were converted.'

HEATING, LIGHTING AND WATER

The Industrial Revolution brought managed heating, lighting, potable water supply and sewage disposal to Britain for the first time. However, the driving factor, to provide power and lighting to manufactories and cottage industries, was not so strong in rural areas, so for much of the 19th century the supply of water, heating and lighting along with the disposal of sewage and rubbish was, in the country, the responsibility of the individual householder.

WATER

Before 1906 and mains supply people relied on the Town Pump, springs, water butts and the river for their water. Every drop used in the home had to be fetched and carried. Meanwhile drovers and carters watered their animals at the river where a slipway by Town Bridge led down to the water. In 1870 the parish erected a pump at the foot of Newton Hill from which farmers could fill their water tanks. It was still in situ in 1955.

The Town Pump was near the old Police Station on the corner of Station Road, which together with wells in The

Row and Church Lane supplied most of the townspeople with drinking water. But they also made heavy use of Green Croft spring, close to the vicarage, which was recognised as providing the best water in Sturminster. Winifred Bradbury recounts how in 1807 the vicar at that time, James Michel, having repaired the spring, decided that it should be used only by his own household because it was on church land. To discourage the townspeople from using it he placed obstacles across the access road. Things came to a head in 1809 when Revd Michel was summoned by disgruntled ratepayers. After much argument and threats of a court action he backed down and allowed the householders free access again.

The late 1880s saw a flurry of legislation that put management of water into the hands of local authorities. Again urban developments were the priority, so it was not until 1906 that work to bring mains supply into Sturminster Newton started. A three-inch cast-iron main brought water from a spring and small reservoir at Church Farm, Ibberton with branch mains laid up Newton Hill to Rolls Mill; to the top of Rixon Hill; also around Church Street and Penny Street. Standpipes were installed at Rivers' Corner, at the top of Glue Hill, at Rixon Hill and at Broad Oak.

ABOVE Laying the water main in 1906.

BELOW Bill King on a return visit with Gwyn Rogers in 1973 to the Lion's Head spring in the grounds of the old vicarage where 60 years before he had taken a drink during a Sunday School outing.

Mr Knott filling up at the pump at the foot of Newton Hill in about 1930. The parish installed the pump in 1870, funded by a halfpenny rate, to supply water to families 'almost destitute of that necessity of Life' (*Western Gazette*, 1870).

In the town cast-iron 'Lion's Mouth' standpipes stood near the Bull Inn, outside Tribe's Clock Shop in Bridge Street, in Church Walk, under the wall below the old school in Penny Street and at Butts Pond. The horse trough outside the White Hart was also connected to the main at one time. It was at this time that a new town fountain and trough was installed at Market Cross to replace the old Town Pump. All the standpipes were dismantled between 1950 and 1960.

With an ever-increasing demand for water in more recent years supplies have been brought in from Alton Pancras and Dewlish.

Sturminster did not get its modern sewage treatment plant until the 1940s. Before this the town drains would have been connected to outfalls into the River Stour. In some cases British rivers became little more than open sewers, creating serious health problems.

GAS

Today gas is pumped to Sturminster through a network of high-pressure mains from many miles away, but once the town had its own gas works, the Sturminster Newton Gas & Coke Company. This was formed in 1864, shortly after the railway came to Sturminster in 1863 – one of the many benefits of this modern transport was a reduction in the price of coal, an essential element in the production of gas. The company was bought in 1914 by Devon Gas

THE GAS MAN COMETH

'From my bedroom window I saw two men from the local gas company repairing a break just outside the White Hart. They were taking it in turns to go into a hole in the road and in a very short while came tottering out again, hardly able to walk because of the gas they had inhaled. They would sit against the pub wall until they had refilled their lungs with fresh air and then down they would go again. This went on for more than an hour, and as a little boy I wondered why they didn't turn the gas off, but of course the old town gas was much heavier than today's and stayed in the trench.'
Reg Cluett, Boyhood Memories of Sturminster Newton, 1996

Association Ltd, which continued in operation until nationalisation in 1949. In March 1953 gas supply to the town came under the Southern Gas Board.

As larger and more modern works made the manufacture of gas easier and cheaper, smaller gas works fell by the way. Gas production at Sturminster finally ceased in June 1957, by which time high-pressure mains had been laid to Blandford and Sturminster from the gas works at Poole.

At its peak, the Sturminster gas works site ran from Penny Street along the west side of Lovers Lane and northwards almost as far as Station Road, and included three gas holders and a showroom that stocked all manner of gas appliances. Gas Works House can still be seen in Penny Street today.

There were two notable by-products of gas production. One was coke, which was sold off to local coal merchants, the other was tar, which was taken to the South West Tar Distillery at Southampton. A more unusual spin-off was 'gas water' which gypsies would use to rub into sore areas on their horses. The local vet also made use of the furnaces to dispose of dead animals – usually late at night – and would cost him 2s 6d.

ELECTRICITY IN THE EARLY DAYS

Before mains electricity, supply was provided by independent generators set up and run as a business by anybody who had the wherewithal. The earliest mention of electricity in the town dates back to October 1924, when Finance & Distribution Corp. won a tender to install 35 street lights.

Sturminster was connected up to mains supply during 1932, following the acquisition of the Sturminster Newton supply undertakings by Wessex Electricity Company in 1931. The town's 11,000-volt supply came from a generating station in Yeovil, via Pulham and Kings Stag before ending up at the back of the last bungalow on the left in Bath Road (opposite the High School). From there an overhead supply fed out into Bath Road and various other transformers around the town. Broad Oak and Glue Hill did not get mains supply until later.

Among the first Wessex Electricity representatives in

The Gas Works at the top end of Penny Street by the entrance to Lovers Lane. (Line drawing by Steve Case.)

town was Fred Weeks who came from Yeovil to succeed Harold Rose. Part of Fred's job was to collect weekly payments from his 44 consumers. If people got behind they were disconnected on the spot by pulling out the fuse.

The initial lure to attract customers to electricity was the promise of three lights and a plug installed free along with up to 30 feet of service cable. For a small extra charge customers could have a choice of two styles of lampshade. Surprisingly many people were still using candles and oil

---

PERSONAL STREET LIGHT

Sturminster's street lights were individually controlled by time switches at various points around the town, and were set to go out at 11 o'clock every night. A certain gentleman in Church Street would phone Wessex Electricity's Fred Weeks from time to time to tell him, 'I aven't got any light and I can't see to undress'. Fred knew the man didn't have any electricity or gas in his house and relied on the street light outside his window near the Chapel. Despite this Fred would still go up to his stores, fetch a ladder and a new lamp, and cycle down to fix the problem.

Guarding the road in and out of Sturminster from Shaftesbury and Child Okeford, this Toll House at Manston still stands (now a private house).

TURNPIKE TOLLS
In an interview with *The Western Gazette* in 1931, Sturminster butcher's wife Mrs Albert Crew, then aged 84, well remembered the turnpike tolls. Her father used to send her into Stalbridge from Lydlinch to buy his tobacco. He gave her 4½d to pay the toll at Stalbridge Gate, but she managed to keep the money for herself by taking a huge detour via the Caundles.

lamps as they felt it was safer than gas or electricity.

As time went on most businesses soon had electricity, although electric cookers in the home took longer to catch on. The first person in the town to have one was the postmaster, Mr Barns, who lived in Bath Road. It didn't take long before four or five orders were placed for cookers, all in the Bath Road area.

ROADS AND TRANSPORT

The River Stour has always provided a penetrating communications route from the south to the north of the county, and the crossing at Sturminster Newton must have been important enough to defend, as witnessed by the Iron Age encampment overlooking this point.

In medieval times road usage was comparatively heavy – goods wagons, pack animals and much foot traffic. But despite the importance of the Stour crossing here (which in all likelihood was a ford opposite the present day Bull Inn), the town did not lie on any long-distance route.

In the 17th century it was recognised that if trade was to grow it was important to have a good road system. Furthermore, the vehicle of long-distance travel, the stagecoach, needed well-maintained roads for the comfort of passengers. Charges levied upon road users were seen as

the most viable way of keeping roads in a good state of repair, and in the early 18th century local Turnpike Trusts were established. Tolls were collected at bars or gates set up at each end of a stretch of road and on side roads linking to the improved road, and these became known as turnpikes.

The first Dorset turnpike road was the Sherborne to Shaftesbury route (roughly the present A30), which received royal assent in 1752. In 1764 The Vale of Blackmore Turnpike Trust started the road across Bagber Common, replacing a route further east. This was followed by the Sherborne to Blandford Turnpike – roughly the route of the current A3030/A357 through Newton and past Town Bridge. Stalbridge Lane, connecting Sturminster to Bagber, Stalbridge and beyond, was a typical old turnpike. The toll gates were at the bottom of Glue Hill, at Bagber, Yewstock, New Cross and at Manston.

The road from the bridge to the town centre, Bridge Street, was little more than a narrow lane, and each time the river flooded the road was inundated. To improve matters, a causeway was built around 1826, raising the level of the road.

The railway with its greater speed and ability to carry far larger loads spelt the end of the turnpike roads and trusts, and in 1889 the main roads and turnpikes became the responsibility of the newly formed County Councils.

With the introduction of motorised road vehicles in the early part of the 20th century, tar was laid on the major roads in the area. Les Ridout, who was working for the Council at that time, recalled that the first road to be surfaced in this way was the A350 from Durweston bridge junction to Blandford.

SOMERSET & DORSET RAILWAY

Imagine being able to catch a train at Sturminster and travel to London, or maybe nip into Blandford without having to take the car. Before 7th March 1966 that is exactly what the residents of Sturminster could do, and much more. Today it is hard to believe that a railway ever ran through the town, so little remains to show for it – only the footpath to Fiddleford, Streeters Carpet warehouse, the brick arches on either side of the River Stour, and, of course, the Railway Gardens that cover the filled-in route of the old railway line itself.

The importance of the railway's arrival cannot be overstated – nor can the tragedy of its demise. The railway brought jobs and prosperity to Sturminster Newton, ushering in the town's heyday. It all began on 1st September 1862 when two independent railway companies – the Dorset Central and the Somerset Central – amalgamated to form the Somerset & Dorset Railway. The first task of the new company was to complete the 16-mile section between Blandford and Templecombe.

In her log book for 10th August 1863, the headmistress at Sturminster Newton Girls and Infants Schools recorded an historic occasion: 'The children very late in the

William Henry Owen retired as stationmaster of Sturminster Newton in 1921 after more than 40 years' service; he was presented with an illuminated address carrying the names of 143 subscribers (now in the Museum) and a cheque for 60 guineas.

afternoon waiting about to see the arrival of the Engine for the first time.' The line was opened to public traffic on 31st August with stations at Henstridge, Stalbridge, Sturminster Newton and Shillingstone.

The railway was a boon to the inhabitants of Sturminster. A wider and cheaper range of goods was available; coal could be brought in more cheaply, which paved the way for the formation of the Gas Company and further benefits; cattle could be transported more easily and thus the livestock market flourished. And it gave people the opportunity to travel further afield for the first time in their lives.

Expansion of the railway system in the south substantially increased traffic, but unfortunately the little S&D was caught unprepared for this sudden demand and soon found itself in financial difficulties. Salvation came in the form of the London & South Western and Midland Railways, which jointly took over the S&D in 1876.

The history of the line mirrors the history of the locality. During the First World War holiday traffic disappeared to be replaced by hospital trains and tank and troop carriers.

A GOAT ON THE LINE

The fireman on a 7F engine saw a goat on the line and told his driver to stop. The fireman got off the cab and caught the goat, which they decided to take on to the next station as the animal was obviously lost. Being a bit of a joker, the fireman thought he would play a game on the signalman at the next box. He put his jacket and hat on the goat and as they approached the box lifted the animal's two front feet onto the side of the cab, then he ducked down. The signalman's face was a picture. He phoned his mate in the next box and said: 'This freight train has just come through, I don't know who that fireman was, but he's got a face just like a goat.'

Alan Hammond, from his book *Heart of the Somerset & Dorset Railway* (2002). Guard Frank Staddon told this story to Gerald Trowbridge, who started work at 14 as a junior porter at Sturminster Newton station in 1944 (Gerald's father Frank was a porter there for more than 20 years.) Gerald passed the tale on to Alan Hammond.

At the outbreak of the Second World War Sturminster Newton station became the dispersal point for evacuees from the big cities. During the war the S&D line was recognised to be of strategic importance as a route between the industrial Midlands and the north and south coasts.

Post war, it was back to business as usual as a thriving market town. Cattle specials were run on a Monday (Market Day), as well as trainloads of chickens bound for

LEFT It was so easy in those days. Mary Clacy sets off for a day's shopping in Bournemouth in the mid 1960s.

BELOW The Sturminster track maintenance team or 'gangers': *from left* Jack Newman, Bill Ware, Denzil 'Digger' Curtis, 'Duchey' Mullens, Albert Snook and Harry Guy.

London. Rail transport was a blessing for other animal breeders. As a young man Peter Elkins, son of miller Sam Elkins, bred prize rabbits. To show them he would simply box them up, put them on the train at Sturminster and 'post' them to shows all over the country. At the receiving end the animals would be fed by the station staff, picked up, exhibited and returned by train in the same way with, it was fervently hoped, their prize cards. Unimaginable these days.

London (via Templecombe) was a favourite destination for passengers. The first train up was the 8.15 a.m., connecting with the 8.51 a.m. at Templecombe and arriving in London at 11.08 a.m. To get back that night travellers would have to leave London at 6 p.m. arriving in

The view from Bonslea House in winter 1963: a train heads towards Stalbridge over the frozen Stour.

Sturminster at 9.23 p.m. Day-trips to Poole and Bournemouth were popular too, and during the summer, excursion trains brought holiday makers from the north to Bournemouth, often running throughout the night.

The first train to Blandford was the 8 a.m., used mainly by workers and school children who would return on the 4.30 or the 6.18. The 6.20 p.m. to Blandford was popular with courting couples, especially on a Friday night. They would have time to see a film at one of the two cinemas, enjoy a fish and chip supper before running for the last train back to Stur. Schoolboys would inevitably get up to some prank or other, and the children sometimes played a rather dangerous game on the railway bridge across the Stour. They would wait for a train to come along, when one would jump in the river and pretend to be having difficulties. The others would stay on the bridge, jumping up and down and waving their arms to attract the attention of passengers. The idea was to try to force the engine to make an emergency stop. It never did and the boys on the bridge would eventually leap into the water to join their friend.

One of the most famous trains on the S&D was the *Pines Express*, which ran from the north of England,

COME DANCING

'Saturdays we all went off to Blandford to the weekly dances at the Corn Exchange. There were always plenty of partners as the army camp was just up the road. We used to catch the 6.20 p.m. from Stur and return on the last train at 11 p.m. If we wanted to go shopping in Poole or Bournemouth, we left Stur at 9.20 a.m. and got into Bournemouth West in less than an hour – the return fare was around 8s. You couldn't do that these days.'

Margaret Score, 2005

The last passenger train: the closure of the Broadstone line to passenger traffic on 7th March 1966 ended 103 years of rail travel at Sturminster Newton. At a packed slide show and talk by David Fox about 'Wold Stur' in March 2006, photos of the station and railway were greeted with audible sighs of nostalgia. The station sign was rescued from a chicken run and is now at the Museum.

through the Midlands, to Bath and then on to Bournemouth. Passengers from Sturminster Newton would have to go to Stalbridge to pick up the *Pines* because it did not stop at Sturminster. There were other interesting trains, among them the Milk Train, nicknamed 'The Blandford Belle', which ran from Templecombe to Bailey Gate (Sturminster Marshall). It was just a passenger train as far as Blandford where it picked up milk and goods; then it ran back from Bailey Gate as a goods-only train (although many people were grateful to a friendly guard to let them ride back).

In the last 10 years of the S&D's life, to 1966, the railway began to look tired and run down. The *Pines Express* was diverted via Oxford and Basingstoke, and it wasn't long before Dr Richard Beeching, chairman of the British Railways Board, was looking at the S&D as a candidate for 'rationalisation' in his grand plan to reshape the railway network.

In 1965 the Minister of Transport in the Conservative government, Ernest Marples, gave consent for the line to be closed. The last passenger train ran on the Somerset & Dorset on 7th March 1966. At Evercreech junction a coffin, covered with blue and yellow wreaths (the colours of the S&D) bearing the inscription 'The Somerset & Dorset died today', was slowly marched onto the Bath train to the tune of 'John Brown's Body'. At 1 a.m. the next morning a mysterious fire destroyed the north signal box at Evercreech junction. And so the S&D railway came to an ignominious end. During its life it had acquired many monikers, such as 'The Swift & Delightful' and 'The Slow & Dirty', but in the end it was simply 'The Sabotaged & Defeated'.

Across the nation, stations were demolished, track lifted, bridges blown up and the cuttings filled in.

THE CANAL THAT NEVER WAS

In the early 1790s a scheme to build a Dorset canal to link Poole and Bristol via the Kennet and Avon Canal in Wiltshire met with widespread approval. It would offer a cheaper and more efficient form of transport for materials such as coal, potter's clay, freestone, lime, timber, slate and wool.

The provisional route ran from Bath to Frome (where there would be a branch that went to the Mendip collieries) and then onwards through Wincanton, Henstridge, Stalbridge, Sturminster Newton, Lydlinch, King's Stag Bridge, Mappowder, Ansty, Puddletown and then from Wareham to Poole Harbour.

Unfortunately, at this point there was a difference of opinion over the route. In addition, landowners affected by the proposals wanted to place their own conditions on the project. The route finally authorised ran from the Kennet and Avon Canal southwards through Sturminster Newton, ending up at Shillingstone – thus the canal's original purpose to link Bristol and Poole had ended in complete failure.

Despite this, eight miles of the canal at the northern end were built and some of its remains can still be seen today. This was deemed to be the most profitable section as it was intended to serve the collieries. Sadly, more problems cropped up and eventually the whole project ran way over budget and ground to a halt in 1803. The final blow was the emergence of the railway network during the 1800s, which dashed any further hopes of rekindling interest in the canal.

The canal idea was resurrected in 1945 when the government proposed a 'Post-War Ship Canal' from Bristol to the Channel and approached local councils for their comments. Sturminster felt unable to lend its support. Nothing ever came of it.

FIRE! FIRE!

With so many thatched buildings, Sturminster has lived constantly with the threat of fire, a fear realised many times. The town experienced a disastrous conflagration in 1681, and in 1729 the centre was again devastated in a fire that destroyed 67 houses, 10 barns and the Market House.

There have also been a couple of memorable fires within living memory. In 1926 Bristol Bazaar, a store at the corner of Ricketts Lane owned by Mr Harding, caught a spark from a passing traction engine. The thatch flared up and the building was destroyed, along with the shop next door

---

FIRE AT KEEPER'S COTTAGE, PIDDLES WOOD

The modern fire fighter is extremely professional, but time was when the volunteer crews faced extraordinary odds – and temptations.

In the early 1900s, the keeper in Piddles wood discovered a fire in his cottage. He ran to alert the fire brigade, going first to Henry Lemon. 'Right,' said Henry, 'We'll zoon 'ave that out. You goo on up and vind Jack Pope, Garge Fry, Garge Pope and the rest of 'em, while I goo out and catch the hoss and put the 'arness on.' Eventually they set off. On the way they had to pass the Bull Inn. The horse, unaware that it was taking the engine to a real fire, pulled in of its own accord. 'Yer,' said George Fry, 'Now we've got this var we'd better 'ave oone vore we do go on up – 'tis going to be a dryish job.'

Having each consumed one pint they decided to drink another, before proceeding on their way. Coming to Black Close Hill, they all had to get down and push, and again when they reached the next hill up to Piddles Gate. On arriving there, they all with one mind suddenly wondered where they were going to get water from. While they had sufficient hose to reach from the road to Keeper's Cottage they only had 10 yards of suction pipe to feed the engine. The nearest water was at the river, some 200 yards down through the wood on the opposite side of the road. Their predicament was resolved, however, by the appearance of the irate keeper. 'Yer, where've you lot bin?' He demanded. 'Cawd, what good is it t'come up yer this time o'day, half boozed at that. There's nothing vor 'ee t'put out now, bar a vew zinders. The best thing you can do is to get back where you've come vrom. You be a vine lot, and that's telling you straight.'

The crew evidently accepted his advice, and it wasn't long before they were back in their favourite rendezvous – the Bull. *Edited extract from a story in The Western Gazette (7th September 1973) by Donald House*

OPPOSITE PAGE TOP The Fire Brigade decked out for an early floral Carnival. Many of the engines bore the words Sturminster Newton Urban District Council despite such a body never having existed. Apparently someone discovered that a Rural District Fire Brigade did not get a financial grant but an Urban District Fire Brigade did.

OPPOSITE PAGE BOTTOM The fire at Barnett's in 1972: within minutes the 18th-century building was ablaze. The fire spread to neighbouring buildings – including a solicitor's, bank and antique shop – but mercifully no one was hurt. The Barnetts lost their home and nearly all their belongings, though they saved three cats, a dog and a canary. The photograph was one of several sold by photographer Helmut Eckardt to raise money for the family. The site was rebuilt and now incorporates the entrance to Market Cross Mews.

occupied by Mr Pope, a shoemaker. The Hardings moved their business down the road to Bridge Street, perhaps unwisely to another thatched building. This too went up in flames in 1956. The shops at Retsel House now stand on its site.

More recently, on 26th October 1972, T.W. Barnett & Son's Hardware Store at Market Cross was totally destroyed by fire. The Sturminster fire crew was joined by colleagues from Shaftesbury, Gillingham, Sherborne, Blandford and Dorchester. The building was a large five-bay house that replaced earlier buildings destroyed in the 1729 tragedy. It says much for the skill of the Fire Service that the thatched buildings close to this incident – a blaze fuelled by paint, paraffin and exploding gas cylinders (some of which landed in the Market Place) – were saved.

Before the advent of fire engines and appliances, the townspeople would fight the fire with water buckets filled from wells and pumps, and pull the burning thatch from the roofs with fire hooks. For example, in Pitts Entry (a narrow passageway between Stour Books and Café Spice) one can still see the chain and hook that once supported a ladder to be used for putting out fires in the thatch. Unless the fire was caught early enough, they could only hope to limit the damage to as few properties as possible. In the case of conflagrations such as that of 1729 very little could be done to halt the progress of the fire.

Eventually, towards the end of the 19th century, the town got its own fire engine, which was stationed in

TOP Bridge Street and Harding's before the 1956 fire.

BELOW 'The fire that engulfed Harding's newsagents shop in 1956 was the news event of the decade. Harding's stood in Bridge Street. As a six-year-old this was on my route to school. I remember picking my way through the mounds of charred beams, thatch and other debris, and the fire brigade hoses strung out across the road. The stench was appalling and stayed with me into adulthood to be rekindled whenever I attended a fire as a reporter. I remember that Mr Harding had carried his young sons Christopher and Richard to safety.' *Roger Guttridge, Dorset Life (March, 1995).*

Church Lane. The late Hector Beale described the contraption as a horse-drawn vehicle weighing about a ton; a crew of at least six worked the pump and would practise in a field by Town Bridge retiring afterwards to the Bull Inn to replenish their spent energy. The horse, tethered to a ring outside which can be seen to this day, waited contentedly with a nosebag of corn.

In 1925, the old engine was replaced by a magnificent new Steam Fire Engine, purchased by Sturminster Newton Rural District Council from the Bryanston estate. The Fire Captain at that time was Arthur Hallett, the clockmaker, whose son Cyril would cycle round to call the fire crew the moment the alarm was raised.

A Merryweather Self-Propelled Pump replaced this engine in about 1933 and was in service throughout the Second World War. In 1941 all fire services were nationalised as a war-time expedient, becoming the National Fire Service. After the war, in 1948, the counties took responsibility for their fire services, and the Dorset Fire Service came into being. This has since been re-named Dorset Fire Brigade.

LAW AND ORDER

In the 18th century and the early part of the 19th century there was no police force as such or public prosecutor. Local constables were appointed by the magistrate on an unpaid basis and played only a minor part in law enforcement. Robert Young recalls that before the establishment of a permanent police force, magistrates selected any townspeople whom they considered fit to act as constables. These unfortunate individuals were expected to take charge of prisoners until the day of their trial. They sometimes took them to a public house where they stood guard over them; on occasions they even took them to their own homes where the prisoners were handcuffed by day and leg bolted by night.

In those days Sturminster Newton's magistrates court was held in the Swan Assembly Rooms. For minor offences, for example theft of goods worth less than a shilling, the typical punishment was designed to humiliate the offender such as exposure in the stocks. For the more serious categories, however, the punishment could be hanging or transportation. At this time it was the responsibility of the victim to prosecute a crime and to pay for all expenses including the apprehending of the perpetrator (the office of Director of Public Prosecutions was not established until 1879).

The first regular police force in Dorset (excluding the boroughs) was established in Sturminster Newton in 1849, with John Hammond appointed as Superintendant at £100 p.a. plus accommodation. The Sturminster Police Station was constructed by 1859 on a site that gave it a commanding view of the three main thoroughfares in the town. The building, which still dominates the Market Place on the corner of Bath Road and Station Road, was designed to be completely self-contained, incorporating offices, stables, cells, living accommodation and a magistrates court. John Hammond went on to become Deputy Chief Constable of Dorset.

These days the Sturminster 'police force' comprises a town beat officer operating from a more modest base in Brinsley Close.

POSTAL SERVICE

The Sturminster Newton Post Office had its premises, from 1895 to 1994, in the building to the left of Lloyds Bank. In August 1994 the business transferred to the One Stop store on Station Road where a dividing wall between the store and a small premises next door (formerly the Spotted Green Dragon toyshop) was knocked down to create space. The Delivery Office (Sorting Office) had already moved from behind the old Post Office to new purpose-built premises on the Butts Pond Industrial Estate in August 1990. There are 15 postal delivery rounds out of Butts Pond from where a team of post people deliver to 5,000 addresses.

The householders of Sturminster come into contact with the post men and women, and indeed the dustmen, groundsmen and street cleaner, on a daily basis, and the town is very fortunate in its friendly and efficient service providers.

STURMINSTER NEWTON LIBRARY

The town did not get a branch library until 1952; until

Outside Triangle Cottage in Goughs Close behind the old Post Office. In 1895 the postmen made three deliveries a day.

then residents had to make do with a few hundred books in locked cases in the Junior School. When the branch library was created its collection was held (not unusually in those days) at a private address, 52 Bridge Street. Today's purpose-built branch of Dorset Library Service in Bath Road was constructed in 1967 as part of the civic complex that included Sturminster Hall and the Police Station (a ramp walkway was added in 2005 to ensure compliance with the Disability and Discrimination Act). It offers 10,600 books, DVDs for rent and much more. There is also a Mobile Library with its own collection of some 5,600 books.

New technology has opened up new opportunities to the townspeople, who have free access to the Internet through the library's computers. The library itself is online and members with online access at home can search the Dorset Library Service catalogue and reserve and renew items in comfort.

STURMINSTER NEWTON CEMETERY

A traveller approaching Sturminster Newton on the Blandford road in 1880 would have seen open land on the left before coming to the Bull Inn, and an uninterrupted view of the river and the bridge on the right. At this time burial space in St Mary's churchyard was almost exhausted. Lieutenant General Augustus Lane-Fox Pitt-Rivers offered an acre south of the river, free of cost, for a cemetery, keeper's cottage and mortuary chapel. The Parish gratefully accepted in November 1880, and work was completed in 1882.

The new cemetery was designated for the burial of both rich and poor of the Parish with no restriction on religious denomination. In laying out the cemetery it was decided to use numbered grave markers in cast iron, with space for a name and date. For those who wished to reserve a particular plot, a cast iron marker would be positioned and the number recorded in the burial book. For the poor who were unable to afford a headstone, the iron marker became the permanent record. There are some fine examples of Victorian markers and head plates in the cemetery.

The first burial was of James Hansford, described as a labourer aged 59, on 10th June 1882. For the first 100 years the average number of annual burials was around 25;

currently it is fewer than 10, including cremations. Of the celebrated names associated with Sturminster, the best known laid to rest in the cemetery is the poet Robert Young (see Chapter 6), who died in 1908. Among those worthy of mention if only for their intriguing names are Tryphena Rowland, Love Turk, Belcher Prebble and Keziah Fudge.

During the Second World War two German aircraft were shot down in the vicinity (see Chapter 4) and the aircrews were buried in the cemetery, on 15th April and 17th June 1941 respectively. The graves were exhumed in spring 1963 and the bodies reburied in the Deutsche Soldatenfriedhof German war cemetery in Cannock Chase, Staffordshire.

Unusually, the Ministry of Supply (Iron and Steel Control) was not able to acquire the cemetery's railings and grave markers during the war years – the Parish Council flatly rejected its attempt in 1941 on the grounds that 'it would not be considered as long as the unsightly dumps of iron around the countryside remained'. The handsome mitred railings around the old cemetery in St Mary's churchyard did not fare so well. These were removed by the Ministry for the princely compensation of £2.13.9d.

There have been two extensions to the cemetery. The first was of half an acre in 1931 purchased from the Rivers Estate for £30. A further 0.6 of an acre was purchased in 1955 at which time a right of way was granted through from Common Lane at 'Four Gates' where there is now an entrance to the car park.

ALLOTMENTS IN STURMINSTER

The origins of allotments stretch back over 200 years to the General Enclosure Act of 1801, which required provision of gardens to be made for the landless poor. Records show that Sturminster had allotments before 1880 (and certainly by the time the first Allotment Act of 1887 introduced the modern concept of allotments): at White Lane (now Bath Road) near the Workhouse; White Lane at Yewstock (three sites); Filbridge Rise; Newton, near the Bull Inn (two sites); and Rivers' Corner. Additional sites were established later: near the bottom of Glue Hill (c. 1918) and two sites near the railway line, at

Butts Pond and Brinsley Close. These 12 sites, totalling 56 acres, were probably all in use at the same time before the 1940s, but were abandoned at various times between 1945 and 1970, with the exception of Filbridge Rise. This site was purchased for community housing from the Rivers Estate in the early 1950s, but only two-thirds were developed; the remainder survives to this day as allotments.

The importance of allotments still remains although the reasons for having them may have changed – from necessity to recreation.

DOCTORS, DENTISTS AND VETS

The town seems to have been well provided for down the years with the services of doctors. The trade directories list a generous helping of surgeons and dentists, and the 1801 Census shows three doctors.

In his memoirs Robert Young tells of Dr James Tarsewell, who lived and had his surgery in Hill House on Bridge Street. The doctor trained his domestic staff to help him in his work: the cook-housekeeper made up the powders and the maid was entrusted to fill small bottles with liquid chloroform which would be applied to an aching tooth; his groom extracted teeth in the stables – a task at which the man was very adept. Overlapping with Dr Tarsewell was Dr John Comyns Leach JP in whose memory the drinking fountain and horse trough were erected. Dr Comyns Leach practised in the town for more than 40 years. He was followed by Drs Hollick and Watts-Sylvester, who also practised here for many years.

The Old Malt House on Bridge Street has for many years been a dental surgery, but in the early 20th century it was a nursing home run by St Mary's Benefit Nursing Association. On St Luke's Day (Luke, the physician) the people of Sturminster would take gifts of non-perishable consumable items down to the home. The nursing home had closed by 1937 and the house reverted to a residential property.

Today a substantial Medical Centre serves the town, offering various clinics and referring patients on to a good choice of hospitals in Dorset, Somerset and Wiltshire. The town has two opticians and two veterinary practices.

NINE

Leisure Pursuits

LIVING IN this rural and relatively isolated part of Dorset, Sturminster people have learnt to entertain themselves. Clubs and recreational activities are an important part of life here, and because of the strong charitable ethos in Sturminster, these are frequently tied into fund raising for local initiatives and charities. The town is unusually lucky in the number of organisations available to its residents.

There is a Leisure Centre and many sports clubs, such as football, cricket, table tennis, short mat bowling and running. As would be expected with such a good fishing river as the Stour, the Angling Association is very active

Happy anglers outside the Mill in about 1960. *From left* Billy Allen, Charles Hayward, Dave Strange, Sam Selby, Michael Selby, (?), Cecil Welch, George Curtis, Harold Hunt, Ted Curtis, Ronnie Welch, Richard Curtis, Bill Mathews, Jack Bennett, Jack Caines, Dennis Barnett, Ray Lane, Edwin Short, Jeremy Barnett.

with more than 400 members. It is impossible to go into detail on every organisation, but the following gives a flavour of what goes on in the town. Contact numbers for these and many more are listed in the community's *Who's Who in Sturminster Newton* leaflet, available from the Town Council, the Community Office and the Library. All of them welcome new members.

OF CARNIVALS AND FESTIVALS

Among the highlights of Sturminster's year are the **Sturminster Show** in June and the **Carnival**, which is held during August. The Carnival draws strongly on the community for organisation and participation and always receives an enthusiastic response. Indeed many local families have been involved with the Carnival for generations. The present series of carnivals dates from 1951, when Sturminster celebrated the Festival of Britain with a children's fancy dress competition and procession of 'decorated tableaux'. Thanks to seed-corn funding from the Parish Council, the Carnival was able to become self-financing and even raise money for local charities.

The first decade of the Carnival was dominated by good-natured rivalry between R. Crew & Son's floral entries and Sturminster Newton Amateur Dramatic Society. But the event evolved over the years, attracting entries from further afield – Hazelbury Bryan, Bishops Caundle and Wincanton. The number of entries varies – the highest being 55 vehicles in 1975, the Carnival's 25th anniversary year. There is no fixed theme, entries are inspired by a wide range of subjects such as current events, popular TV programmes or traditional themes such as nursery rhymes. All this gives the event a friendly and spontaneous atmosphere. The early one-day Carnival has grown into a week-long series of events and competitions that culminate in the fancy dress and procession. Over the years the Carnival has raised a huge amount of money, which it has distributed to local causes.

A more recent initiative is the annual **Cheese Festival** in September. With the closure of the livestock market in 1997, a small group of volunteers decided that it was important for the town to retain its market identity, so the festival was conceived to promote the Milk Factory's famous Sturminster Cheddar Cheese. Sadly, in 2000 the factory too closed, but the Cheese Festival continues to grow, and the two-day event, attracts some 8,000 to 10,000 visitors from far and wide.

ABOVE The Daleks invade Sturminster during Carnival 1965.

THE ARTS

In 1841 a Literary and Scientific Institution was founded in the town, and the townsfolk continue to have a keen interest in the arts. The **Arts Appreciation Society** was formed in 1971 by a handful of people who wanted to listen to classical music. Monthly meetings expanded to include coach trips to concerts, plays, opera and ballet. Membership is well over the 200 mark. Club Nights include enthusiastic speakers and the occasional musical evening, mostly CDs but sometimes a 'live' musician. No speaker has ever failed to turn up, but the club keeps a quiz up its sleeve just in case.

The town also has its own **Choral Society**. Its roots go back to 1957 when the WI asked a young music master at the High School, Alan Hannah, to form a choir. The singing at a Christmas pageant in 1962 was of such a high standard that Mr Hannah took the opportunity to set up a choral society. Its first concert, part of Handel's 'Messiah', was held in December 1963 in St Mary's. Twice-yearly concerts of sacred music, at Christmas and in the spring, have continued ever since under Mr Hannah and various other conductors, including George Havord, Cecil Cox, St Mary's organist Peter Lattimer and Barry Ferguson, and

LOOKING FOR FOSSILS IN COOMB

'The foot path across the fields, that started behind the Minister's house by the Newton Hill Methodist Chapel, joined a small lane, one of the few places for spindleberries. To the left was the wooded valley known as Coomb with a brook that flowed round Castle Farm down to the Stour near the Bull. A small bed of watercress showed the water was very clean. In winter the brook ran high and fast, washing out little sea-urchins and bivalves from the yellowish Corallian limestone upstream from the footbridge from Glue Hill to Broad Oak. When the water was low, fossils collected on islands of gravel along the stream-bed – a Jurassic park without the dinosaurs. School summer holidays meant expeditions to look for fossils, fuelled by lemonade and sweets. When we got bored with the hunt there were badger setts to inspect with their old bedding, foot-prints and mud slides for the cubs. On one visit I came face to face with a young fox coming up a grassy rise, we stared at each other in surprise. The fox turned and trotted quietly away.'
Denise Le Voir (née Barnett), 2005

Sturminster Choral Society in 1965: *back row from left* Kerry Minnear, Keith Goddard, Steven White, Edward Pope, Ken Jones (chairman); *fourth row from left* Peter Lovell, Garry Minnear, David Cross, Brian Downer, John Fish, (?), (?), (?), Edmond Nash; *third row from left* Aileen Winkworth, Deany Yeatman, Isobel James, Harriet Clarke, (?), (?), Esther Sutherland, Nancy White; *second row from left* Felicity Minnear, Mary Hall, Honey Staniland, Joyce Gurney, Muriel Tong, Mrs Duffett, (?), (?), Kath Green, Pam Donaldson, (?); *front row from left* Vi Tuffin, Vera Fisher, Mary Kent, Eileen Daybourne, (?), Alan Hannah (conductor), Muriel Minnear (accompanist), Miss Marlen, Miss White, Mrs Waller, Connie Young.

with accompanists Doris Edsall, Mike English and Elaine Korman.

Local men enjoyed singing so much that in 1994 they set up the **Mill Singers**, a male voice choir of about 20 members with a wide and varied repertoire, much of it unaccompanied. Initially it drew from the Sturminster area but now attracts members from other parts of Dorset. Under the musical directorship of Peter Lattimer, and sporting distinctive red bow ties, the men pursue high musical standards and the choir is much in demand in the county and in Montebourg, Sturminster's French twin town. Performances over the years have raised more than £20,000 for charities.

St Mary's Church boasts a fine peal of six bells, which are rung regularly by a small but enthusiastic band of **Bell Ringers**. They meet to practise on Wednesday evenings and ring regularly for the Sunday services and for weddings. They work in close co-operation with ringers from Lydlinch and Marnhull, adding to the social value of their meetings. Ringers from far and wide regularly visit the

ABOVE John Pruden and Ray Rogers, the Ugly Sisters in SNADS' 1968 performance of 'Cinderella', written and devised by Harry Dawes (junior) and produced by Molly Weston.

BELOW The Male Chorus strut their stuff in 'Dick Whittingon', SNADS' 1983 panto: *from left* John Cowley, Daryl Weyman, Robert Cowley, Clive Gray, Peter Cowley and Andrew Davis. The Male Chorus first got together for SNADS' Queen's Silver Jubilee entertainment (1977) and was such a success that it has been a feature of the panto ever since.

ABOVE SNADS stars in the 1966 production of Joan Coates' 'Moonshine' in the Hut: *sitting from left* Pat Moody, Felicity Minnear, Molly Weston, Margaret Warham; *standing from left* Sheila Dyer, Garry Minnear, Ann Allen, Roger Hammond.

church to compare Sturminster's peal of bells to others, and members visit other towers.

Amateur dramatics have been at the heart of town entertainment for well over 100 years, and since its inception in 1930 **Sturminster Newton Amateur Dramatic Society**, affectionately known as SNADS, has been one of Stur's most energetic groups. In the early years after the war, the regular venue was the Comrades Hut in Bath Road (now the British Legion), where SNADS would assemble its portable wooden platform and trestles and play to large and eager audiences. The repertoire increased when Ron and Molly Weston arrived from Swanage with their experience of pantomime. SNADS put on its first panto, 'Dick Whittington', in 1955. Ron Weston and Harry Dawes (junior) wrote the script, starting a tradition that has seen most of the pantomimes penned by local writers. Panto audiences have been known to exceed 1,220 in a week. SNADS has been a stalwart of the Carnival, frequently winning the coveted Championship Rose Bowl in the days of spectacular tableaux.

With the opening of Sturminster Hall in 1967, SNADS has had a permanent stage, usually offering two plays and a pantomime every year. There have been festival entries and the occasional touring production – one play was taken to Guys Marsh Prison. The society continues to be involved in local events, the opening of Sturminster Museum in 1989 and the millennium celebrations in 2000 for example. A new chapter opens with The Exchange, which will provide SNADS with a stage and storage under one roof.

But the quality of a society lies in its members. The names of Sturminster natives and long-term residents who got together in 1946 are now part of history. Their numbers were augmented by returning servicemen and women and then by a steadily changing roll of bank clerks, teachers and others passing through or moving in. Acting members are essential, but many more bodies are involved behind the scenes. SNADS has a large membership and brings together a wide variety of people who enjoy each other's company as well as putting on plays and entertaining thousands of people over the years.

GREEN FINGERS

In such beautiful rural surroundings it is not surprising that the town should field both a Floral Group and a Horticultural Society. The **Floral Group**, founded in 1964 by Lady Paquita Morshead, comprises around 30 to 40 members. It holds an annual Flower Show in May when members compete in eight classes for prizes and three cups. Every year a different charity is chosen to receive a donation from the profits.

The **Horticultural Society**, founded by Harry Dawes (senior), was suspended at the start of the Second World War and resurrected in January 1978 by his son Harry, who held the post of secretary for 24 years until 2002. There are monthly meetings when experts are invited to speak and demonstrate. There is also a show of members' produce, flowers, fruit, wines, domestic items, floral arrangements and photography in July.

Lady Paquita Morshead, founder of the Floral Group.

BRANCHES OF NATIONAL ORGANISATIONS

Honourable mention goes first to the **Women's Institute**, whose co-operation has been instrumental in making this book possible. The Sturminster Newton branch has played an important role in the life of the town particularly through wartime (see Chapter 4), and continues to thrive after 85 years with more than 30 members. Meetings are held on the first Tuesday of the month, except August when there is an outing or picnic; it also holds a monthly lunch club, and sometimes organises theatre trips. The WI always enters a team for the Hall Quiz and also the County Whist event. Its teas, put on at the request of other organisations, are legendary. Several Sturminster members attend the National Federations of Women's Institutes Conference, which is influential at national and EU level on issues such as the environment, consumer affairs and public affairs in general. The Monday WI Market at the British Legion Hall is now called the Country Market.

Along with the WI, Stur boasts branches of many other national and international organisations. The Sturminster Newton Branch of the **Royal British Legion** was formed in 1921 from what was known as the Old Comrades

ABOVE The WI's prize-winning Carnival float in 1984: *sitting from left* Queenie Gibbs, Madeleine Barber, Mrs Hawthornthwaite, Renee Moore, Peggy Hatcher; *standing from left* Mrs Hudson, Joan Pitts, Antoinette Britt, Lillian Gushlow.

Association. This had been set up in 1919 by Colonel William Douglas Whatman to assist the men returning home from the First World War. Colonel Whatman was the branch's first president, assisted by Charlie Stride as secretary. He arranged for a wooden hut to be brought from Blandford Camp in 1919 and erected on Bath Road. 'The Comrades Hut' became the headquarters of the branch, and the site remains so to this day. In its time it has served as a social club for ex-servicemen and as a cinema. When it was first opened, Bob Hatcher, a local war hero who had been awarded the Military Medal during the First World War, was appointed steward, a post he kept until he took over the Red Lion pub in the mid-1940s. The branch looks after the welfare of ex-service personnel and their dependants, primarily through the Poppy Appeal, which it has co-ordinated in the town since its launch in 1921. It also takes the lead in organising Remembrance Services in the town.

In the uncertain days of early 1944, when preparations were underway for the Normandy landings, a group of local businessmen and professional men voted to form a

Rotary Club to serve the local community. Herbert Allen, manager of the National Provincial Bank, was elected the first president. Of the 23 founder members, Albert Hammond and Wilfred Bailey were grandfather and father respectively of two of the present-day members. In 2004 the Club celebrated its 60th anniversary as a member of Rotary International of Great Britain and Ireland. Early community work included offering transport from Templecombe Station to stranded service men and women returning home on leave, financial support for the Girl Guides' camping outing and a Christmas treat for the residents of Stour View House – an apple and sixpence. Times have changed and these days the Rotary motto of 'Service Above Self' continues in other forms: Life Education mobile classrooms; emergency aid boxes for rapid response to major disaster areas; the eradication of polio; mock job interviews for students leaving the High School; and support for the Sturminster Show, the Cheese Festival and the Dorset Steam Fair. The Club also organised the funding, exhibition and selection of the statue to commemorate the site of the old livestock market.

A few months after the USA came into the First World War, a Life Insurance Company executive in Chicago, Melvin Jones, along with a few Christian friends felt they should help the families whose menfolk were sent to France to fight, and often to die, in the trenches. A convention of like-minded businessmen in Texas in 1917 resulted directly in the formation of 37 service clubs across the States. The idea spread rapidly, first into Canada, then

Sturminster Newton's Scout Group was founded in 1924.

through all the Americas and China. The **Lions** clubs did not reach Europe until after the Second World War. Lions stands for 'Liberty, Intelligence, Our Nations Safety'. Its motto is 'We Serve'. Membership is open by invitation to service-minded people over the age of 18 of all races and faiths. The **Lions Club** of the Blackmore Vale, formed in 1979, is fairly typical of the 1,000 or so clubs in the UK: a membership of around 20, composed of people from a wide range of backgrounds. It holds two business meetings a month in a Vale village to discuss requests for assistance

---

ELEPHANTS IN THE STOUR
'Grandma Newman lived at Butts Pond. I would spend quite a number of weekends with her. The fair field was opposite her house; fairs would arrive and sometimes animal shows. Being in bed and hearing the lions roar, seeing the animals in their cages – it was all a thrill. They would take the elephants to Town Bridge to the river to drink. One time they came back, several women were gossiping outside the Rivers Arms and the elephants squirted water all over them.'
Hilda Lilian Hatherley (née Rose) was born at Glue Hill in 1908. From her recollections for the WI history of Sturminster.

A rainy-day outing in June 1926: the Mothers Union sets off to Swanage.

from individuals and other charitable organisations, and to plan fund raising and social activities. People in the Vale generously support the annual Swimarathon, Half Marathon, Grocery Draw and the Blackmore Vale Walk, while Father Christmas tours the villages and hamlets on his float during December. Thanks to these activities, to its members and to support from the Lions Ladies, the club passes on about £13,000 a year to those who most need it, as well as offering help in the form of time and energy.

The Sturminster Newton detachment of the **British Red Cross Society**, known as Dorset 18, evolved from the disbanding of the wartime Air Raid Precautions. To start with it comprised enthusiastic First Aiders who asked to set up a detachment. Further First Aid and nursing training was undergone and a Junior Red Cross Unit set up at the High School. The detachment ran a 24-hour Medical Loan Department (now running smoothly from Gillingham), and still runs an ambulance staffed by trained members, at local school, carnival and horse trial events. It operates from various premises as required since it had to give up its Bath Road centre because of asbestos in the roof.

The **Silver Thread Club** was formed in 1950 by members of the local Red Cross to give the elderly an afternoon out and a meeting every two weeks. This continues today as a club for the over 60s. It meets in the Hall every other week on a Thursday afternoon. Silver Thread also organises outings to places of interest and

speakers on various subjects – and tea and biscuits, of course.

The **1st Sturminster Newton Guides** hold activities and challenges that aim to develop self-awareness, self-respect and self-confidence. The unit has about two dozen members aged between 10 and 17 years. The 14 to 16 year olds call themselves the Big Gs and mentor younger Guides, often organising and leading evenings. Summer Camp can be a lot of fun but the girls learn about tolerance and leadership as well. Weekly meetings offer a programme of learning opportunities, such as new crafts, impromptu drama and cooking on camping stoves, balanced with developing an understanding of broader issues, such as world cultures and the environment. In 2005 there was a 'homeless evening' when the guides discovered first-hand the discomforts of living in a cardboard box as they constructed their own shelters and 'busked' for their chip supper.

The **Mothers' Union** was founded in 1879 to bring together mothers of all classes to train their children in Christian family life. Today it is a worldwide organisation. The date of the founding of the Sturminster Newton

Sturminster St Mary's Football Club, 1907-08, winners of the Shaftesbury and District Minor League. *Back row* E.P. Dunham (hon. sec.), J. Rose, J. Cluett, J. Drake (selection committee), R. Matthews, B. Fudge; *middle row* H.R. Cressey, J. Northover, A. Hussey (captain), M. Lemon, H. Cluett, S. Cressey (selection committee); *front* E. Wood, J. Allner.

Revellers pour into Stur in 1966 for the Carnival procession.

branch is not known, but according to the earliest surviving record book, it already had some 45 members by March 1916. Its banner, ordered in 1939 and fairly frail now, hangs in the north transept of St Mary's and is still taken to festival services. In 1974 the members of Salisbury diocese bought two caravans at Durdle Door campsite to let out to families who otherwise could not afford a holiday. These have been replaced by a modern six-berth mobile home which branch members still take their turn cleaning. They have also helped run a family holiday on the Isle of Wight. Local families have benefited from both projects. By 1980 the branch had become involved with helping to run a 'tuck shop' for prison visitors at Guys Marsh, and these days serves teas and coffees in the Visitors Centre there. For many years it has had a link with the MU in Lusaka, Zambia and sends Easter and Christmas presents. In 1995 the branch was put into abeyance, but reformed in 2002 with the arrival of the Revd David Seymour and meets every month. It recently helped buy a Virtual Reality Baby for the High School.

SPORTING LIFE

Since 2002, Sturminster has had its own **Leisure Centre** (off Honeymead Lane), funded and managed by North Dorset District Council. It boasts a gym, an aerobic studio and a sports hall. The centre offers regular exercise classes, yoga, spinning and a variety of games, among them badminton, basketball and indoor cricket.

Football was first played in Sturminster in the early 1870s, by a team that called itself the Panthers. The town now has two teams: Sturminster Newton United Football Club and Sturminster Rovers.

In 1873 the Panthers entered the FA Cup and recorded their best victory in the competition beating Wood Grange 3-0. In the 1890s the influence of the church took over and the club changed its name to Sturminster St Mary's, a name it kept until 1945 when the club decided to call itself **Sturminster Newton United FC**. The club was a founder member of the Dorset Combination League in 1957, but had to withdraw in 1960 because of financial problems. Over the next decade the team played in the Dorset League. The club really took off in the 1970s and '80s with tournaments on the Continent. SN United remained unbeaten through a total of 14 matches against teams from Holland, Belgium, France and Germany. 1972 saw a return to the Combination League after winning the Dorset League Division One, but the team had to wait nearly 10 years for further success when in 1981 they beat Wareham to win the Combination Cup. In 1995 they won the cup a second time, defeating Sherborne 2-1. 1996 was another memorable year when the club moved from the Recreation Ground to its own ground at Honeymead Lane.

Formed originally as a team of locals playing in a charity game in May 1991, **Sturminster Rovers FC** came into being after joining the Blackmore Vale Football League in June 1991. (Sturminster Football Club had already had a side in the BVL for several years.) After considerable opposition, the Rovers were forced to play their home games at Hazelbury Bryan, where they played for two and a half seasons before moving to Hinton St Mary. In 1997 the team reached the final of the Merthyr-Guest Cup and moved their home venue to the Recreation Ground. The following year they won their first trophy, the McCreery Cup. In 2002 the Rovers won Division One of the BVL and in 2003 took the McCreery Cup again. At the end of the 2004-05 season the team were relegated to Division Two, but were top of the Division by the end of October 2005.

The **Ladies Hockey Club**, not far off its 30th season in 2006, fields three teams at weekends, and has recently won the league for the third consecutive season. The club has a successful junior section. Both ladies and children train on Wednesdays at the Clayesmore Astroturf.

THE MUSEUM SOCIETY

Finally, a word about the **Museum Society** itself. The spur for establishing a museum in the town was the sudden death in 1984 of Raymond Rogers, who was the Registrar for North Dorset. He had been passionate about local history, a keen campaigner for a museum and left behind a large collection of artefacts and photographs. His friends and associates took up his baton, and in August 1984 the Sturminster Newton Museum Society came into being with elected officers, a draft constitution and its registration as a charity. The former Union Workhouse Chapel in Bath Road, by then owned by Dorset County Council, was proposed as a site, and in early 1986, DCC agreed to lease the chapel to the Town Council which sublet it to the Museum Society. Members of the society set about gaining public support and raising funds for the extensive repairs and alterations needed to make the chapel suitable as a museum. Much of the repair work was done voluntarily; in particular, Stanley Score, a friend of Ray Rogers, devoted his spare time to restoring the chapel. Following Stan's death in 1987, the proceeds of his memorial fund paid for some essential work and brought the opening of a museum closer. The efforts of Stan, Ray and Tom Fox, who was also keenly interested in local history, helped to establish a core of archival material with which to start the museum's collection. Sturminster's museum was finally opened on 15th July 1989 by Agnes Williams, a granddaughter of Montague Williams, who had built the chapel in 1890. The grand opening was accompanied by Morris dancers, bell ringers, a car boot sale, a town crier and much attention from the press.

In 1994, the Town Council asked the Museum Society to take over the running of Sturminster Newton Mill, which had been left idle for some years (see Chapter 1). The mill is owned by the Rivers Estate which leases the site to the Town Council. The mill and museum are now managed by the Sturminster Newton Museum Society and run by volunteers.

TEN

Folklore, Myths and Legends

STURMINSTER is rich in tales of strange happenings. There are those who feel this might have something to do with the town's location on the route of an ancient ley line linking Stonehenge to Bind Barrow near Burton Bradstock. The ley line passes through the Market Cross, Town Bridge and the castle site. The following is a selection of the many tales in circulation and draws from sightings both past and present.

Certainly, Sturminster has its fair share of haunted buildings and houses. The ghost of a 'grey lady' has been seen (though not recently) walking through the bar area of the White Hart. People have seen other apparitions too in the old Union Workhouse in Bath Road (now the Stour View Family Centre). One of the ghosts was a Mrs Bowsden who would walk the passages towards the old library; another was a ginger cat which stalked the building; and the ghost of a baby would prompt older residents at the centre to warn 'mind that baby crawling on the floor'.

Another haunting is, reportedly, at Market House (now Root & Vine) where a little chimney sweep who refused to do his job was thrown into the cellar and chained up as punishment. The ghost is not that of the boy but of his mother, who can be heard running through the building in response to her son's rattling chains.

The Swan Inn, meanwhile, has a happy ghost on its premises, although the story is a sad one. The sudden death of a former landlord caused much sadness as he was a friendly and well-liked fellow. But he was soon back at the inn where, apparently, he remains to this day. He is said to be friendly and the staff call him George. The Bull Inn at Newton, too, has a ghostly resident – an old gentleman smoking a pipe, who has made a spectral appearance on several occasions.

A pipe-smoking apparition has put in several appearances at the Bull Inn (photo c. 1930).

TRAGIC BACKDROPS

Great tragedies affecting communities often become a backdrop to local stories. One such was the terrible fire in Sturminster in 1729.

A house in the centre of the town was said to be haunted by the ghost of a woman who had died there. Once a year, on her wedding anniversary, the apparition would appear to haunt her husband. She would walk upstairs to his room carrying a lighted candle and place it outside his door before entering the room herself. The 1729 fire coincided with the couple's wedding anniversary. The house was destroyed in the blaze and the husband was found lying dead in his bed, not a single burn upon his body. Among the smouldering ruins, the candle was found, still alight, exactly where the ghost was said to place it. It remained alight until the body of the husband had been laid to rest alongside that of his wife, when it finally went out of its own accord.

A similar story concerns a house haunted by a man who, in the space of three months, had lost his three children and his wife. He became deeply bitter, and he shunned society. He was often observed walking silently around the house carrying a candle. On the third night of every second month he could be seen carrying a candle into the porch where it was left to burn all night. People believed that he was worshipping the Devil. When he died, the house was occupied successively by three families. Each left after seeing the candle and hearing the stories of a ghost. After the house burnt to the ground in the 1729 fire a lighted candle could still be seen burning in the place where the porch had been. It was only extinguished when it had burnt itself out.

TOWN BRIDGE

The Town Bridge area is the setting for a number of supernatural encounters, two of which are recalled below in the words of the person who experienced them. Both took place in one of the old cottages that still exist near the bridge.

'I was sitting in the dining room, which was part of a new extension to the property. As I looked towards what was originally the kitchen, a woman appeared from nowhere. She turned right as if going to where the sink or the back door had been. The figure wore a long flowing grey dress. She appeared so real that I thought it was my friend's wife and I was very surprised when I found out that it wasn't. On another occasion I was sat upstairs, as before, in the new part of the house. As I looked over towards the landing, near the old staircase, the lady in grey appeared again. She did not seem to be aware of my presence and, after each encounter, she simply vanished.'

In August 1965 the bridge was the scene of a tragic accident when a Mini collided with a heavy lorry and the three occupants of the Mini were killed. About a year later, a boy was passing the spot on his motorbike when three people suddenly stepped out into the road in front of him. Unable to stop, he rode right into them, but passed straight through the figures. When he looked back they had completely disappeared.

BURIED TREASURE

Much folklore (and wishful thinking) has grown up around the site of the castle. There are said to be valuable treasures in a nearby well, although unfortunately nobody knows where the well is. Legend also has it that a large object of solid gold is hidden inside a secret tunnel. In different versions, this is a table, a throne, or in some accounts, a replica of King Arthur's mythical Round Table. The tunnel is said to run between the castle and the mill, and at certain times the ghost of a monk may be seen following this route down the side of the hill.

This may not be the only tunnel leading to the castle. There is recorded and anecdotal evidence to support the existence of four such routes. The one mentioned above is the shortest tunnel; the longest apparently runs all the way to Okeford Fitzpaine; a third goes to a point near Rivers' Corner; and a fourth finishes just outside Piddles Wood at Leigh's Clump (a rectangle of elms long since gone). Leigh's Clump is said to have been haunted – the site is variously reputed to be a hunting lodge used by King John, a burial ground for victims of the Black Death, and a Civil War camp used by Charles I (under the name of King Charles' Ring).

THE NEWTON LION

On the porch roof of the Red Lion public house in Newton was an effigy of a lion couchant, painted red. Each night, at the stroke of midnight, it would dismount from its plinth, stroll down to the old pump near Town Bridge and have a leisurely drink from the Stour before returning. Many drinkers on their way home after an evening at the Red Lion said they had seen it – some say they even saw two!

Next to the Red Lion was a cottage with a doorknocker that was said to knock of its own accord every night. Apparently the owner had died leaving a sum of money to various charities, but his daughter went against her father's wishes and kept all the money for herself. Every night there would be knocking on the door until the daughter could bear it no longer and paid the money to the charities. From that moment on the knocking ceased. The door is no longer there as the cottage has been incorporated into the property next door and the doorway has long since been blocked up.

THE PHANTOM STAGECOACH

On 15th April 2002, a local farmer was out ploughing between Bagber and Newton beside an old green lane used

The Red Lion (c. 1880): the lion sometimes hopped off its plinth and went walkabout at midnight.

in bygone days. It was a quarter past midnight when he first saw what appeared to be smoke. He checked for engine trouble, exhaust fumes and even a bonfire nearby, but found nothing. By now the smoke was all around him.

'I suddenly noticed a strange glow coming from the corner of the field on the other side of the hedge, moving along the lane. I could clearly make out the shape of a stagecoach, like in the old western movies. It had a square door and a shaped front window. I could even see the ridge along the top where the occupants would have put their baggage. I couldn't make out any people or horses and there was no sound other than that of the tractor engine ticking over. Unfortunately I could only see the top three or four feet as the rest of the coach was obscured by the hedge. The coach continued down the lane behind me until it was almost level with me. At this point it reached a large oak tree – but never reappeared on the other side. It, quite simply, disappeared. The next day I went back to see if there were any tracks left in the lane, but there was nothing to be seen.'

The story doesn't quite end there. When the farmer returned home that night his girlfriend asked if somebody had been up in the field to visit him as she'd seen a bright blue light on the skyline going down the green lane towards him. She thought it might have been a vehicle but the light had disappeared immediately behind the tractor.

Plumber Manor, scene of a legendary tragedy. These days the manor is run as a hotel and restaurant.

The farmer was not the only person to have seen the stagecoach. Fifteen years earlier a woman who used to live in Bagber was driving on the A357 when a stagecoach appeared to be coming straight towards her.

THE HOUNDS OF PLUMBER MANOR

There are many variations on the next story, but this account appears to be the oldest and most commonly held version of events.

Just south of Newton lies Plumber Manor, the home, since around 1660, of the Prideaux-Brune family. There, a room adjoining the gallery is known as the 'Haunted Room'. One night, the then Lord of the Manor was woken by the baying of his hounds as they fought fiercely among themselves. Clad only in his night attire, he rushed out of his bedroom, through the gallery and down the stairs. He tried desperately to separate the hounds but to no avail. Instead, they turned on their master and tore him to pieces. Next morning, all that remained of the much-respected lord were his two thumbs. From time to time, it is said, the ghost of the master rushed through and out of the house to the accompaniment of baying hounds. But rest easy, there hasn't been a sighting for many years.

FOUR GATES

On the way to Broad Oak, near the entrance to the Sturminster Cemetery car park, is an area known as 'Four Gates' because of the four gates that used to be there. This spot was apparently the site of a murder committed many years ago. The story goes that a sailor on furlough had been out drinking in one of the inns at Newton. He had a considerable amount of money on his person and when he left he was followed. At Four Gates he was set upon and killed. People still tend to steer clear of this place after dark and some local residents refer to the first left hand bend on the road to Broad Oak as 'Dark Corner' and will hurry by 'just in case'.

The ghost of a man carrying a loudly ticking watch may be heard if not actually seen at Four Gates. He is thought to be Job Rose, who worked at the cemetery sometime in the late 19th century and whose journey home took him to Four Gates, across Coomb and finally to Glue Hill. Every evening, when the church clock chimed 7.30, he would pack up his tools and wind his way home, pausing only at Four Gates to hear the church bells ring out the 8 o'clock curfew. Then he would take out his hunter watch (a rare and expensive item in those days) and check the time before carrying on home. (In olden days a curfew was rung out as a signal to put out all fires and lights: in more recent times it was rung to let the workers know that it was time to stop work.)

ROAMING ROMAN

The village of Hinton St Mary lies on the northern approach to Sturminster and is where one of Britain's finest Roman mosaics was discovered in 1963 in the remains of an ancient Roman villa. It was carefully removed and taken to the British Museum. Not long after, a strange apparition began to appear, walking around the excavation site – the ghostly figure of a Roman, dressed in a tunic. To this day, he can be seen roaming around his old home – or so they say.

THE FLYING DONKEY

Further south, off the Bath Road is Honeymead Lane, now quite built up but once just another quiet country lane. One misty night, a young woman was making her way home when she saw a donkey pulling a cart outlined against the fog and suspended in mid air. In the cart stood a young lad, whip in hand, desperately urging the donkey

Once upon a time there were two old spinsters, known locally as 'the wormies'. Their family name was Ridout, and they shared a cottage just below the churchyard. They earned a living by making rush mats and church hassocks. The spinsters never associated with anyone and were said to have the 'evil eye': they practised charms and would hang up a bottle containing frogs' entrails and a bullock's heart stuck with pins inside the old wide chimney to prevent witches from entering by this route.

For some reason they thought that the village schoolmaster had bewitched them. The only remedy that could break this spell was to draw some of the poor man's blood, which they did by scratching him with a pin when next they met him in the street. Unfortunately nobody recorded what happened afterwards but the schoolmaster cannot have been very impressed.

Sadly, both of the spinsters were found dead one day in the snow by Haydon Farm near Plumber, and for many years two crosses marked the spot in the hedgerow.

There has long been a bakery at the site of the current Sturminster baker's where a ghost occasionally makes his presence felt.

to go faster. As she watched, the image vanished into thin air. When she got home and told her mother what had happened, her mother became very upset. Years before a young boy, who used to drive a donkey cart, had been brutally murdered at the very same spot.

THE TALE OF THE MILKMAID

These days we tend to put such stories down to a failure to understand things that can now easily be explained. Yet people continue to have experiences that are difficult to rationalise.

Early one November evening in 2004 a woman was driving into town when a ghostly female shape appeared near Town Bridge. From the apparition's features and apron, it was quite clearly a milkmaid. The driver, by now somewhat shaken, continued to her destination where she described the experience, expecting to have her story dismissed. She was more than taken aback when she learned the following. In 1947 Vera Dymond lived with her parents in Keeper's Cottage, a house that used to be in the middle of Piddles Wood. Vera was a milkmaid and she worked on a farm in Stalbridge Lane. One day she was cycling down Newton Hill, near the mill, when she lost control of her bike. She was thrown headlong over the handlebars and killed outright. The story goes that she had been carrying a container of milk and, despite the sudden impact of the collision, not a single drop of milk was spilt.

THE BAKERY GHOST

Another more recent manifestation concerns Sturminster's bakery, at the top of Bridge Street. Members of staff report seeing the spectre of a man, hearing a voice and feeling someone tugging at their sleeve. One interesting aspect is that just before he appears staff might get an itchy nose, feel cold or notice a smell of pepper. Fortunately the ghost seems quite friendly and has even been seen relaxing in a chair.

TOM DEWFALL

No chapter about strange happenings in Sturminster would be complete without the Tom Dewfall stories, told by the late Olive Knott in *Pictorial History of Sturminster Newton*. The first takes place when the Somerset & Dorset

ABOVE Rixon Hill (c. 1900) where the ghost of Tom Dewfall appeared to a young woman and her children.

Railway was still in operation and was recounted to Miss Knott by a friend.

'I was returning home one evening in late spring, pushing a pram with my baby in it and her sister aged three holding my hand. When we reached the station hill, I saw a man who had evidently come off the train. I recognised him as a friend who had emigrated to America, Tom Dewfall.

"Hello, Tom," I called out. "I didn't know you were in England. I suppose you've come to liven up the election?" (Tom had always been very keen on electioneering and was an ardent Tory). Tom made no reply but motioned as if to say "Don't talk to me." Then he laid his hand on the pram and walked with us until we reached the top of Rixon Hill. My little girl was chattering all the time and didn't seem to notice how silent Tom was. I went into one of the cottages to tell a relative that Tom Dewfall had come again. When I came out he had gone.

Next day I stopped at the cottage where Tom usually called. His friend was standing at the door. I called out that I had seen Tom the previous night. "Oh no, you didn't," the other replied, "I had a letter this morning to say that poor Tom had passed away." "What!" I cried. "He came off the train and walked with me to the top of the hill." Then I realised why Tom hadn't spoken and why he had vanished.'

A few years later, during the Second World War, a number of children from the Blandford Grammar School were to be evacuated to the USA, among them the daughter of the woman who had told the story about Tom Dewfall. The girl was to join a married daughter of Dewfall's who had settled in America. Her clothes were packed and her passage booked when both the girl's parents had the same nightmare, in which Tom Dewfall appeared wringing his hands and shaking his head. The father interpreted this as a warning: 'We mustn't let the maid go to America.' And they didn't. They cancelled the booking. Later, they heard that the *Lusitania*, the boat in which the girl was to have sailed, had been torpedoed and sunk. They attributed their daughter's escape to the timely warning of Tom Dewfall's ghost.

Hair-raising stuff! But either the name of the ship or the date of the story is incorrect: the *Lusitania* was in fact sunk on 7th May 1915. (These inaccuracies have been dealt with thoroughly in two books, *Mysterious Dorset* by Rodney Legg and *Oral Folk-Tales of Wessex* by Kingsley Palmer.) One would, of course, like to believe that both tales are true and that the recollection of dates and names has simply been a little confused.

ELEVEN
Links to the Wider World

IT IS EASY to assume that Sturminster Newton and its preceding settlements have nestled in the heart of the Blackmore Vale unknown to and unknowing of the outside world. This, of course, is far from true. Evidence now suggests that even Iron Age settlements traded goods from the Continent. Sites of local Roman villas suggest the Romans were comfortably settled in the immediate area for two or three hundred years.

By 1790 Sturminster was raising several hundred oxen each year to send far beyond the Vale. Most were driven to Smithfield, and the ox drove still exists, climbing up from Melbury Abbas and running eastwards for many miles. The drovers of that time are named as John King and George and William Lambert. Farmers near Sturminster were also sending 10 tons of butter each week to Poole for shipment to Southampton and London, the carriers being Richard Northover and the Foot family, Henry, John and Thomas.

For centuries smuggling was a way of life for a section of Dorset's community (see Chapter 1). Contraband would be brought ashore at night and the small barrels transported well inland by daybreak to be hidden in farm buildings and mills. One such smuggling gang, the Ridout family, was centred on the villages of Fiddleford and Okeford Fitzpaine. They would have needed trusted contacts across the Channel and crews who knew every inch of the coastline. Legitimate trade and fishing also flourished, and Coker's *Survey of Dorsetshire* tells us that the ports of Lyme, Bridport and Weymouth were busy in the early 17th century, as was Poole, an extremely important port from the 15th to the 19th centuries. Every port needs a hinterland to produce exports and absorb imports.

SWANSKIN

It is somewhat surprising to find that Sturminster Newton, situated some 25 miles inland on an unnavigable river had close ties with the sea. But quite apart from day-to-day trade and smuggling routes, there was another, stronger connection: Swanskin, the tough, waterproof, felt-like woollen cloth produced exclusively in and around Sturminster (see Chapter 7). After John Cabot's voyage of discovery to the 'New world' in 1497, the rich fishing grounds off Newfoundland began to be exploited; exploitation led to mainland settlements; settlements meant trade; trade meant merchants. As Newfoundland's cod fishing industry flourished so did Sturminster's Swanskin industry, providing warm, all-weather clothing for the fishermen on the high seas and cold, foggy fishing banks.

A Newfoundland bride: Catherine Penny was brought back to this country in about 1880 as the wife of Richard Penny.

A steady stream of people followed the trade across the Atlantic over the years. In fact, so many people from Sturminster and other parts of Dorset settled in Newfoundland that even today the Dorset dialect can be recognised across the province, and it is reckoned that in the scattered north coast fishing communities of Twillingate some 45 per cent of their ancestors came from the Blackmore Vale. Fertile, black Dorset soil can still be seen in the rocky landscape – carried from Poole as ship's ballast. The link with this area is also reflected in the number of Sturminster area surnames to be found in Newfoundland: Ridout/Rideout, Hancock/Handcock, Young, Penny/Penney, Clark/Clarke, White, Parsons, Barnes, Butt, Rose, Hillier, Fudge, Rogers, Ford, Yeatman/Yetman, Caines, Short, Upshall, Dyke, Curtis, Hart, Snook, Hammond, Gillard, Hatcher, Burden, Drake, Cuff, Stockley, Ricketts, Porter, Warren.

Professor Gordon Handcock of Newfoundland's Memorial University, himself a descendant of Sturminster Hancocks, writes in his book *Soe Longe As There Comes Noe Women: Origins of English Settlement in Newfoundland* (Breakwater Books): 'By place of marriage, we can link Sturminster natives with over 25 Newfoundland settlements, but they were strongly represented in Fogo and Twillingate, Carbonear, and especially the district of Fortune Bay and westward to Rose Blanche.'

The weavers of Sturminster were very much the bottom rung of the ladder. *The Universal British Directory of Trade and Commerce* 1790 states: 'The principal manufactory carried on here is for white baize or swanskin; in which the poor, who are very numerous, are chiefly employed.' The same directory also tells us that the William Williams Charity paid out 'weavers money' from the White Hart Inn every three years. Some local people, however, profited from the trade with Newfoundland and became merchants, among them families of Hasketts, Forwards, Birds and Colbournes. The will of Thomas Colbourne of 1820 (a copy resides in the Museum) bequeaths well over £10,000 in cash to various relatives, a considerable sum in those days. Ambrose, Charles, George and John Forward all left Sturminster in the late 1700s and

created a dynasty of master mariners, ship owners and general merchants in Newfoundland, amassing considerable fortunes in goods, ships, properties and so on.

At this time, the end of the 18th century, the mills at Sturminster seem to have been in the hands of the Newman family, with Joseph and Samuel Newman being fullers together with Thomas Swain; John Newman and William Harrison being the grain millers. By the early 1800s, however, faced with industrialisation in the north and increased competition, the Swanskin trade rapidly declined, and in the space of two decades it had disappeared.

AUSTRALIA

On 8th August 1992 a ceremony took place in Sturminster that re-united local and Australian members of the Rose family. At Port Jackson in Australia a similar ceremony was held on 15th January 1993. These events marked the 200th anniversaries of the departure from England and subsequent arrival in Australia of Thomas and Jane Rose and their children. The part they played in 'opening up' that country is fairly well known locally but not outside the Sturminster area.

From soon after its discovery, Australia was used solely as a penal colony, fit only for convicts and their guards. This continued until the early 1790s, when the governor, Arthur Philip, appealed to the British government to send 'free settlers' to found an independent productive community. No doubt he saw the advantages of being more self-sufficient and less dependent on convict labour and supply ships with five-month-old cargoes.

Only 14 people responded to the appeal: six men from various parts of the country, at least some of whom had served in the army as guards of the prison colony, and a group of eight from Sturminster Newton. This latter party comprised a local farmer Thomas Rose and his wife Jane (née Topp), their four children, their niece Elizabeth Fish and her friend Elizabeth Watts. The whole party left Gravesend on 8th August 1792 aboard the *Bellona*, a supply ship which also carried a number of women convicts. It eventually reached New South Wales on 16th January 1793.

All the settlers were given free passage and on arrival were granted land near Liberty Plains in New South Wales, tools, basic provisions, clothes and the use of convict labour. The Roses' fifth child was born here. But poor soil conditions and lack of local climatic and seasonal knowledge meant they faced several very difficult years. In 1794 one of their fellow travellers, Thomas Webb, was killed by an aboriginal spear. The Rose family was also attacked and only her whalebone corset saved Jane from a spear. Thomas and Jane had two more children and in 1802 moved further inland to farm better land at Wilberforce (not far from Sydney) near the Hawkesbury River. But again lack of local knowledge resulted in the loss of their possessions in a series of floods. Undaunted, and after building several temporary wooden shelters, they chose a spot on higher ground and erected a sturdy wooden dwelling which became known as Rose Cottage. This cottage, extended over the years, survives as a museum piece having continued in family ownership until 1961.

Jane died in December 1827 and Thomas in November 1833, having been the first family to settle in Australia of their own free will. Jane was the first free settler to have a child in Australia and subsequently the first settler to become a great grandmother. Rose Cottage is the oldest settlers' home in Australia and was the venue of the first Methodist service in Australia held by the Revd Samuel Leigh. The cottage is now looked after by the flourishing Thomas and Jane Rose Society, which keeps in contact with Sturminster Newton Museum Society.

Another important branch of the Rose family followed Thomas and Jane to Australia some years later. Reuben Rose was born in 1819, the fifth of nine children of a farm labourer. Although the parents, Benjamin and Sarah, were baptised, married and buried in Sturminster the family moved from farm to farm a number of times, all within a few miles of their home town. These were grim times for Dorset labourers as witnessed by the unrest in Tolpuddle in 1834 and elsewhere. Reuben Rose in Sturminster was a teenager at the time. He would have been aware of how the first Roses had fared in Sydney and of the opportunities that beckoned. In 1843 Reuben married Hannah Jeanes of

Rose Cottage, Thomas and Jane Rose's home in New South Wales.

Stalbridge, and in 1849 they emigrated with their two children to South Australia, where they settled first at Glen Osmond before moving to Watergate, near Macclesfield, also in South Australia. Reuben and Hannah were very successful in their adopted homeland and a further seven children were born to them. Their many descendants have formed another Rose Family Society

THE FRENCH CONNECTION
Sturminster Newton celebrated the 10th anniversary of its twinning arrangement with the Normandy town of Montebourg in 2004. An arrangement with L'Aigle had previously existed through Sturminster's Rotary Club, so it was not until August 1991 that a meeting chaired by Town Council chairman Archie Meaker decided to find a link town of equivalent size in Normandy.

Representatives from Montebourg visited in March 1993, and in April an open meeting in Sturminster gave the go-ahead. Progress then was rapid. There were fund raising events for twinning expenses; representatives from Sturminster went to Montebourg and dined with the mayor; and the following February a Sturminster delegation led by Frank Lane, chairman of the Twinning Association, comprising his wife Jan and two daughters, association secretary Gill Turner, Geoff Clacy and Matthew and Jenny Price, made a first visit to Montebourg's Chandeleur (Candlemas fair). Local farmer

ABOVE Montebourg twinners at the Tithe Barn in Hinton St Mary celebrate the 10th anniversary of the twinning arrangement with Sturminster Newton. *From left* Gérard Demoulin, Marilyne Lecampion and Bruno Le Cacheux (president of the Montebourg Twinning Association).

Bob Green, working with the NFU, arranged a visit of 15 French farmers in April 1994 and a return trip was made that September. The farmers still exchange visits.

Twinning agreements were signed in September 1994 and April 1995. The Sturminster Newton Twinning Association presented the French with a model of St Mary's Church by R F Southwell and later a framed picture of the mill by Brian Moore.

The Chandeleur is a magnificent annual fair and Sturminster twinners have done their best to support it with a stand of produce and items from the town. It is always hoped that trade between Normandy and Dorset

BELOW Triumphant Sturminster twinners carry home the coveted Boule trophy on 15th May 2005 aboard the Cherbourg/Poole ferry. *Back from left* Jeremy Read, Joe Rose (town councillor), Fran Rose, Maurice Williamson, Revd David Seymour, David Cornes; *front from left* Luise Cornes, Helen Lamper (secretary), Janet Bolton (Boule captain), Vic Bolton, Bob Green (chairman of the Sturminster Newton Twinning Association).

will benefit from the twinning, and indeed some English farmers have shown interest in buying maize from France after seeing their trials. In 1997 the French brought cider, Calvados and cheeses to the Shop Show and sold out within three hours.

Musical events have enriched exchanges over the period. The Montebourg band came over for the Carnival in 1995. In the same year, the local Mill Singers sang for an audience of 300 and made a recording in the Abbey at Montebourg. The singers make regular trips to France.

School exchanges had already been taking place through the Rotary's French connection, and these have continued since through the Twinning Association. A high point was in 1998 when a group of 44 from the High School attended the Chandeleur and undertook several weeks of work experience with local firms.

The game of Boule has been taken up by some twinners with enthusiastic support from their French friends. The landlord of the Plough at Manston made a terrain and since then a terrain has also been made at Fiddleford. In 2004 Montebourg donated a magnificent trophy to be competed for at exchanges. Sturminster and Montebourg enjoy a friendly rivalry in various other sports – football, skittles (which the French often win), cricket (which usually ends in chaos) and tug of war.

The 60th anniversary of the D-Day Landings was commemorated with a talk by Twinning Association chairman Bob Green on the liberation of Montebourg in 1944. This account revealed the appalling damage and casualties inflicted on the town, which had been largely untouched during the Occupation.

To celebrate the 10th anniversary of the twinning in 2004, a large delegation came from France. Among the entertainments was a party at the Tithe Barn, Hinton St Mary, at which the Montebourg guests were introduced to the very English pastime of Beetle Drive. The following year the guests reciprocated with a pear tree, which was planted at the Hinton Memorial Garden. In May 2005 Sturminster presented Montebourg with a seat bearing a brass plaque, which has been placed in the town's public garden.

THE TALENTED FULLERS

Although the town seems curiously unaware of it, Sturminster was the launch pad for the musical career of a talented group of young people who achieved considerable fame in America. Towards the end of the first decade of the 20th century, Walter Fuller, his wife Elizabeth and their five children settled into Bridge Cottage, Sturminster. They were hoping to make a fresh start after the failure of their Portsmouth drapery business. Of the children, Walter (junior, aged 27) was at university; Oriska (25), known as Riss, had studied the harp and was a graduate of London's Royal College of Music; the other three girls, Dorothy (19), Rosalind (17) and Cynthia (14), had little formal education but all loved anything creative and especially the folk songs their mother taught them.

Moving into the Blackmore Vale countryside seems to have been a catalyst for the girls. They immediately formed 'The Sturminster Newton Pastoral Players'. Their folk singing quickly established a considerable local reputation because no less a person than Cecil Sharp, the great authority and collector of folk music, came to Sturminster to hear them. A chance remark by an American friend of Sharp's about taking their music to the United States was seized upon, and very soon Walter and his sisters were making plans.

Their parents appear to have indulged the children's every creative whim, believing them to be 'special' even if not exactly appreciating the extent of their talents, and a trip to America was agreed. Young Walter would be manager, compere and chaperone, Riss would play harp, Dorothy, with her strong mezzo-soprano voice, would be lead singer, and Rosalind would also sing and 'do the actions'. Cynthia would stay at home.

Two seasons of hard work followed to raise money for the adventure. Encouraged by the Revd Mansel-Pleydell, they performed *A Midsummer Night's Dream* in the Swan Assembly Rooms, *A Masque of the Seasons*, which they wrote and performed in the Swan and in the vicarage garden, and *Merrie England* (the masque rewritten as a pageant) with a cast of more than 80. These players included many familiar local names: Master Alfred Cluett, Misses Rosie Inkpen, Olive Strange, Agnes Burt and Hilda

King, Mr Ernest Knott, Mr A.R. Clarke and Miss Eva Knott. Master Cyril Hallett played a cuckoo and Miss Winifred Cluett was the Harvest Moon.

In December 1911, armed with Victorian costumes, a letter of introduction from Cecil Sharp, one-way tickets and enough money to last a fortnight, the young Fullers set off for America. The first tour was a great success, playing mainly for the 'at homes' of the rich and famous, but increasingly to schools and colleges.

Soon after their return home in May 1912, Riss married one of Walter's friends and Cynthia, now 17, took her place as harpist. A second tour (January to June 1913) followed, then a third (September 1913 to May 1914) and fourth (October 1914 to April 1916). During the second tour they sang at the White House for President Woodrow Wilson and also at his country home in Vermont. As the tours progressed Walter and his sisters became increasingly independent. They sang anti-war (First World War) songs and became greatly interested in the feminist movement. Walter, weary of searching for bookings and balancing accounts, remained in America after the fourth tour and secretly married a leading militant feminist.

Back home, Riss led a 'Votes for Women' march through Sturminster and Rosalind went to London to chain herself to the railings of Buckingham Palace. Meanwhile local people threw bricks through the cottage windows in protest at the fact that a friend of Walter's, Curt Dehn, was half German by birth.

A fifth tour went ahead (October 1916 to September 1917), but the Fuller sisters' ideals were now out of step with the general mood of the American public, and on their return the family began to drift apart.

Walter became editor of *The Radio Times*, but died at 47; Riss played harp in the BBC Northern Orchestra; Dorothy married surveyor and musician John Odell and illustrated children's books; Cynthia married Curt Dehn and became an artist. Rosalind joined the Folies Bergère and went on to become a leading Broadway actress; she returned to the London stage, where her leading men

Three of the Fuller sisters on their first tour of the United States: *from left* Rosalind, Dorothy and Riss.

included Donald Wolfit, Richard Burton and Emlyn Williams. She was awarded an MBE for services to the theatre. The original Irish harp has emigrated with some of the family to Australia.

TWELVE

Today and in the Future

*'Sturminster may be a small market town,
but it's a great place to live!'*

STURMINSTER NEWTON is the kind of place where people will greet each other even if they are strangers – a courtesy that has changed little down the years but is getting increasingly rare as communities expand and lose their identity. There is a natural feeling of interest in and concern for others in Sturminster that has grown up over time. It's a valuable quality and one that could so easily be lost.

Nowhere of course remains immune from the effects of modern life. Greater affluence and mobility, advances in communications, increasing levels of noise, a faster tempo yet a seemingly shrinking number of hours in the day – all lead to stress and strain. So far Sturminster has managed to accommodate most of this 'progress' without losing too many of its essential values. But the previous chapters indicate how times have changed, and continue to change.

The town has had to recover from major losses: the Somerset & Dorset Railway; the Sturminster Rural District Council; the livestock market; and the Milk Factory. Massive residential development is significantly increasing the population, and the accompanying weight of traffic into and through the town is becoming a serious and unpleasant problem for everyone.

Yet Sturminster has an indomitable spirit, and this manifests itself in many different ways. The town is blessed with a large number of gifted and dedicated people, both local and incomers. Their initiative is responsible for many of the imaginative and successful businesses in the area, and their inspiration is behind the huge array of clubs, societies and associations (see Chapter 8) that are active in the town.

The arrival of a dedicated community worker for the town and the surrounding area when the livestock market

Sturminster Newton Hall in 2005. The hall was opened on 17th March 1967, made possible by bequests of land and money from Sidney Knott, fund-raising by local organisations and personal donations. It is replaced by The Exchange in the town's market site development.

An artist's maquette of the six-ton Portland stone column for the redeveloped market site, its four faces commemorating Sturminster Newton's market history. The project was devised by the local Rotary Club, with the help of the Arts Council, to mark the club's 60th anniversary in May 2004, and enthusiastically supported by the community. Four artists were invited to put forward their ideas to an exhibition and public meeting. The people of the town voted for Peter Griffin's proposal (above). The main funding came from the Arts Council.

closed has seen the emergence of a new community partnership involving a wider range of committed local people. Together with a pro-active Town Council and other local authority bodies, they have worked tirelessly to produce serious and achievable plans for the future of the town and surrounding villages.

It is largely as a result of this significant increase in community activity that Sturminster now has:

• SturQuest, the Community Partnership – an organisation supporting initiatives that local people feel should be pursued.

• Unity.Com – a free monthly magazine, delivered to every household, which keeps the community informed about local activities and matters of importance.

• The Community Office – a central point where information and assistance on a range of local affairs is available.

• The Exchange – a new building, purpose built to accommodate events and activities large and small, market activities, the Town Council and the Community Learning Centre.

• SturStat – a prominent sculpture representing Stur's past and future, including the vital contribution of the livestock market.

• NORDCAT (North Dorset Community Accessible Transport) – an organisation with a fleet of small buses that take people from their homes to where they need to go, either regularly or on request.

• The Cheese Festival – a two-day open-air event each September that brings together producers to display and promote the great variety of delicious foods that are manufactured locally.

Along with the development of the old market site, a new road layout has enabled expansion of the town centre to include The Exchange building, a new Medical Centre and supermarket. The Jubilee Path will be a safe and pleasant traffic-free route into the centre from the new housing developments to the north; and the North Dorset Trailway will provide an off-road connection through the countryside south-east towards Blandford and north-west towards Stalbridge re-using the trackbed of the old railway. Meanwhile Butts Pond Meadows has been

The timeless Blackmore Vale. A view taken by Charlie Stride from Shillingstone Hill in 1930.

lovingly transformed by volunteers into both a nature reserve and a valuable amenity area in the heart of the town's new residential development.

There is a great deal to be proud of, and to look forward to. 'Sturminster,' says an experienced local councillor, 'has now begun to get back the voice in its own future that had been lost in recent years.'

But time does not stand still, and challenges lie ahead. The population of the town at the 2001 Census was 3,110. The Town Council put this figure at 3,300 in 2006 and expects it to rise to 4,300 by 2008. This growth brings new potential, but it needs to be matched by facilities and services.

Thankfully, Sturminster is still a safe and attractive environment in which to bring up young children. But as they grow older, their interests broaden and their needs increase. These will have to be properly addressed.

If the age range of the community is to remain in balance, then suitable employment locally will always be a priority. The potential is there for businesses to be established at the designated business park at Rolls Mill.

We all know something of the enormity of the revolution that is still taking place in agriculture, and how fundamentally it has changed lives and livelihoods in this rural area. But the countryside that surrounds us is a precious asset, and ways will have to be found to ensure its continued wellbeing.

From the heights of Bulbarrow or Okeford Hill, the breathtaking beauty of the Blackmore Vale spreads out before the 21st century observer much as it did for Thomas Hardy. It is a view that allows a wider perspective of the challenges Sturminster Newton faces: to remain faithful to the eternal values embodied in the real and enduring world of the land, the perpetual rhythm of the seasons and the weather, and to acknowledge our own place within all of this.

And if, at the same time, this small community can steer its way through the increasing frenzy of the modern world to grow and develop at a steady and appropriate pace, then it has every chance of remaining the place where people will continue to feel contented, fulfilled and welcome.

Bibliography

'Alfred the Great', Wikipedia, the Free Encyclopedia [online, accessed April 2006]

Archbold's Parish Officer (1858)

Arnold-Baker, Charles, *Local Council Administration* (1984)

Ashdown, Douglas, 'The Reverend William Barnes', *William Barnes of Dorset*, William Barnes Society (2001)

Asser's Life of King Alfred (Simon Keynes and Michael Lapidge, trans), Penguin Books (1983)

Atthill, Robin, *The Somerset and Dorset Railway*, Pan Books (1970)

Austin, Frances and Bernard Jones, 'William Barnes and the Schools in Sturminster Newton', *William Barnes of Dorset*, William Barnes Society (2001)

Bartelot, Richard Grosvenor, *Vanished Mediaeval Castles of Dorset*, Proceedings of the Dorset Natural History and Archaeological Society (vol. 66) (1945)

Baxter, Lucy, *Life of William Barnes, Poet and Philologist* (1887)

Beaton, David, *Dorset's Forgotten Heroes*, Dovecote Press (2005)

Bettey, Joseph Harold, *Wessex from AD1000*, Longman (1986)
Man and the Land: 150 Years of Dorset Farming 1846-1996, Dorset Natural History and Archaeological Society (1996)
Farming, Dovecote Press (2000)

Biggs, Barry John, *The Wesleys and the Early Dorset Methodists*, Woodsorrel Publications (1987)

Billett, Michael, *Thatched Buildings of Dorset*, Robert Hale (1984)

Bond, J., *Monastic Landscapes*, Tempus (2004)

Boswell, Edward, *The Civil Division of the County of Dorset* (1833)

Bowden-Smith, Mrs Harold (wife of the vicar of St Mary's Church), memoirs (c.1950)

Bradbury, Mary, *Steadfast in Faith* (1997)

Broad Oak Community Orchard, Dorset Wildlife Trust

Brown, Lionel, *The Story of the Dorset Congregational Association* (1971)

Brown, Mary, *Dorset: Customs, Curiosities and Country Lore*, Ensign Publications (1990)

Butler, David, contribution to *The General Election of 1945* (1948)

Camden, William, *Britannia* (1607)

Campbell-Kease, John, *The History of Hazelbury Bryan* (1983)

'Cheese Please', *The Bridge Magazine* (December 1994)

Chorley, Bill, 'Wartime Crashes at Sturminster Newton', *Aviation News* (February 1989)

Clacy, Geoffrey, 'The Passing of an Era', *The Bridge Magazine* (July 1994)

Clacy, Mary, *Agriculture in the Blackmore Vale*, research at Sarum St Michael, Salisbury (1967)

Cluett, Reginald W., *Boyhood Memories of Sturminster Newton* (c. 1996)

Coker, John, *Survey of Dorsetshire* (by Thomas Gerard under the name of John Coker from his mid-17th century manuscripts) (1732)

Collier, Clive, *Southern Electric: A History* (1992)

Countryside Guide to North Dorset, North Dorset Rangers

Cunliffe, Barry, *Wessex to AD1000*, Longman (1993)

Dacombe, Marianne R. (ed.), Members of Women's Institutes, *Dorset Up Along and Down Along*, C.J. Creed (1935)

Day, John C., *Once Upon a Time in Sturminster Newton* (1999)

Densham, William and Joseph Ogle, *Congregational Churches of Dorset* (1899)

Domesday Book, Old Sturminster Newton, Dorsetshire.com [online, accessed April 2006]

The Dorset & Somerset Canal, Inland Waterways Association

Dorset County Guide (1956)

Dorset Natural History and Antiquarian Field Club, *Field Meeting Notes (un-attributed), 22nd September 1903*, Proceedings (vol. 24) (1903)
Proceedings (vol. 16) (1895)

Dorset Natural History and Archaeological Society, *Proceedings* vol. 100) (1978)

'Dorset Tithe Protest', *Western Gazette* (24th February 1933)

Drew, Charles, *The Charles Drew Index*, Dorset County Museum

Durkin, David, *Report on a 14th Century Manor House Set within an Iron Age Hill Fort*, dissertation report, University of Bristol (2004)

The Electronic Sawyer Anglo-Saxon Charters, 'Wills and Bequests (S 1507)' (revised edn by S E Kelly), British Academy and Royal Historical Society (1991) [accessed April 2006]

Eyton, Robert, *A Key to Domesday* (1880)

Finberg, Herbert Patrick Reginald, *Studies in Early English History*, Leicester University Press (1964)

'Foot and Mouth Disease in Great Britain', *Annual Report*, Agricultural Department, Privy Council Office (1883)

Forty, George, *Frontline Dorset, A County at War 1939-45*, Dorset Books (1994)

Gates, Doreen and Joyce Cundle, 'Sixty Years', *Dorset Times* (September 1999)

'Girl Guidance', *Interlife Magazine* (issue 02, 2005)

Good, Ronald, *Old Roads of Dorset* (1966)
The Lost Villages of Dorset, Dovecote Press (1979)
The Great Chartulary of Glastonbury (iii 592-3 no. 1095), Somerset Record Society (vol. 64)

Gunnell, Clive, *Secret Dorset*, Bossiney Books (1995)

Guttridge, Roger, *Blackmore Vale Camera*, Dovecote Press (1991)
Dorset Smugglers, Dorset Publishing Company (1987)
'Stour Valley Heritage', *Stour Valley News* (13th April 1996)
'Literary Sturminster Newton', *Dorset Life* (September 1998)

'Roger Guttridge's Wessex Heritage', *Blackmore Vale Magazine* (10th December 1999)
'Sturminster Newton's Newfoundland Connection', *Dorset Life* (April 2006)

Hall, Olive A., *Where Elm Trees Grew: Fiddleford in Dorset*, Castle Cary Press (1988)

Hammond, Alan, *Heart of the Somerset and Dorset Railway*, Millstream Books (2002)

Harold, Mary, 'Piddles Wood Nature Reserve', *Dorset* (October, 1998)

Hearing, Terry, *Dorset Justice*, Magistrates' Association, Dorset Branch (1999)

Holt, Richard, *Medieval Mills of England*, Oxford University Press (1988)

House, Harry, *Harry John House 1898-1971: Some Stories from His Early Years*, Sturminster Newton Museum (1989)

'Houses of Benedictine Monks: The Abbey of Glastonbury', University of London and History of Parliament Trust, British History Online [accessed April 2006]

Hudson, James William, *The History of Adult Education* (1851)

Hutchins, John, *The History and Antiquaries of the County of Dorset* (3rd edn, vol. 4, 1861-1870) (1873)

Irving, E.M., 'Wartime Memories', *The Bridge Magazine* (November 1993)

Jackson, Amy M., *The History of the Dorset Button* (1970)

Jones, Irene, *The Stalbridge Inheritance 1780-1854*, Larkwood Publishing (1993)

Joyce, Ray, *The Golden Age of Poole Dorset* [videotape], in association with Poole Museum Service (2000)

Kelly's Directory of Dorsetshire 1885, 1915, 1927, 1935, Dorset Record Office

Kerr, Barbara, *Bound to the Soil: A Social History of Dorset*, Dorset Books (1968)

Knight, Peter, *Ancient Stones of Dorset*, Power Publications (1996)

Knott, Olive, *Dorset with Hardy*, Longmans (Dorchester) (1968)

'Hardy's Sturminster Home', Appendix by James Stevens Cox (ed.), *Monographs on the Life, Times and Works of Thomas Hardy*, Toucan Press (1968)

'Sturminster Newton in the Old Days', *The Dorset Year Book 1971-72*

Tales of Dorset, Friary Press (1976)

and Raymond Rogers, *Pictorial History of Sturminster Newton*, Dorset Publishing Company (1973)

Lane-Fox Pitt-Rivers, George, *The Story of the Ancient Manor of Hinton St Mary*, Pitt-Rivers Museum

Legg, Rodney, *Dorset's War Diary*, Dorset Publishing Company (2004)

Mysterious Dorset, Dorset Publishing Company (1998)

Matthews, Rupert, *Ghosthunter Walks in Dorset*, S.B. Publications (2004)

Methodist Church, Sturminster, *Methodism in Sturminster Newton* (1982)

Millennium Time Walk 2000: A Community Pageant [videotape], JECK Films

Mills, Anthony David (ed.), *The Dorset Lay Subsidy Roll of 1332*, Dorset Record Society (vol. 4) (1971)

Moody, Pat, 'What's in a Name?', *The Voice of the Churches* (November 1994)

Moore, Brian, 'I've Enjoyed the Journey,' *Dorset Life* (August 2005)

Moore, Rene and Sylvia Rose, *Children Evacuated During the War* (1992)

Morshead, Owen Frederick, *The Story of the Parish Church of St Mary, Sturminster Newton* (1971)

Ordnance Survey, *25 inches to 1 mile Survey* (1st edn, 1873)
25 inches to 1 mile Survey (2nd edn, 1902)
1:2500 Survey (1980)

Palmer, Kingsley, *Oral Folk-Tales of Wessex*, David & Charles (1973)

Parsons, D., *What Is a Good Egg? A Guide for Candlers, Packers and Egg Producers*

Perks, Frederick, *Mereinhylle: The Biography of the Dorset Village of Marnhull* (1983)

Piddles Wood Nature Trail, Dorset Wildlife Trust (2000)

Roberts, A.W.M., *Farming in Dorset* (1979)

Roscoe, Ernest (ed.), *The Marn'll Book*, Blackmore Press (1952)

Royal Commission on Historical Monuments (England), *An Inventory of Historical Monuments in the County of Dorset* (vol. 3, Central Dorset, part 2) (1970)

Saunders, Tim, *A Brief history of Dorset's County Yeomanry*, Keep Military Museum, Dorchester (2003)

The Queen's Own Dorset Yeomanry and 5th Battalion the Dorset Regiment: Gallipoli 1915, Keep Military Museum (2005)

Sawley, Ruth, *Roses All the Way*, Mushroom Graphics (1986)

Scott, G.R., *The History of Rinderpest in Britain, Part One 809-1799*, State Veterinary Journal (vol. 6) (1996)

Snook, Catherine, '377thC Remembered', *Sturminster Tymes* (August 1997)

Strange, J.W., home-made films (1938-45)

Steven Cox, James, interview with Mrs Mabel Ellen Penny, February 1966, appendix to Olive Knott's 'Hardy's Sturminster Home', Toucan Press (1986)

'Stur Market Ending this Month', *Blackmore Vale Magazine* (20th June 1997)

Sturminster Cheeses feature, *Dorset Evening Echo* (February 1979)

Sturminster Newton Area Guide and Map, Senior & Godwin (1958)

Sturminster Newton Guide (1977)

Sturminster Newton Tourist Guide (2000)

Sturminster Newton Women's Institute, *A History of Sturminster Newton* (1983)

Sturminster Newton Women's Institute, *Silver Jubilee Book* (1965)

Sturminster Rural District Council, *Brinsley Court* (September 1968)

Syddall, Penny, 'Market Holds Town to Ransome', *Western Gazette* (14th September 1995)

Taylor, Christopher, *The Making of the English Landscape: Dorset*, Hodder & Stoughton (1970)

Toulmin-Smith, Lucy (ed.), *The Itinerary of John Leland in or about the Years 1535-1543* (parts 9, 10, 11), G. Bell & Sons (1910)

Townsend, Hilary, *Blackmore Vale*, Dovecote Press (2004)

Waring, Edward, *Ghosts and Legends of the Dorset Countryside*, Compton Press (1977)

Watts, Martin, *The Archaeology of Mills and Milling*, Tempus Publishing (2002)

Weinstock, Maureen Bessie, *Old Dorset*, David & Charles (1967)

Whitcock, Ralph, *Dorset Farming*, Dovecote Press (1982)

Whitfield, Chris, 'Mondays Will Never Be the Same Again', *Dorset Life* (September 1997)

Wildlife of the River Stour, Environment Agency (1998)

www.dorsetforyou.com [accessed April 2006]

www.nicolathorne.co.uk [accessed March 2006]

www.sturminster-site.net [accessed April 2006]

OTHER SOURCES

John Alexander. J.J. Armfields' drawing of the Mill (1904). Stephen and Karen Blake. Tony Butler. Joe Casey. Stan Clarke. Tony Cottrell, Master Thatcher. Betty Cowley. Robert Cowley. Avril Cross. Percy Curtis, Ted Drew and George Lydford (personal interviews by Alan Harrison, May 1984). Norman Damerell. Barbara Danoris. Dorset Historic Churches Trust (online). Dorset Countryside. Dorset History Centre. Dorset Wildlife Trust. Nicki Edwards. Mary Fish. David Fox. Paul Giles. Phyllis Goddard. Ernie Gorge. Connie Guttridge. Hampshire Record Office. Alan Hannah. Ken Harvey. Jim and Peggy Hatcher. Hebe Howard (letter to BVM, 20th May 2005). Gordon and Michele Henderson. Barry 'Dizzy' Hiscock. Humberts (sales particulars for Sturminster Newton Market, August 1989). Keep Museum staff. Lois Kernaghan (family history research, 1974). Eve King. Ken Knott. Simon Moody. John Musto. Esmé Newman. Carol Odell (daughter of Dorothy Fuller), family history research, 2005. Rivers Estate Office Rental Records. Anthony Pitt-Rivers. Premier Livestock Auctions (Sturminster Newton Throughput Figures 1969-1996). Norah Puckett. Alan Rigg. Gwyn Rogers. Thomas and Jane Rose Family Society. Rotary Club of Sturminster Newton. Rural Action for the Environment. Salvation Army *War Cry*, Karen Thompson and staff of the Salvation Army International Heritage Centre, London. Margaret Score. Sam and Helen Selby. Staff and pupils of Sturminster Newton High School past and present, and school magazines. Sturminster Newton Library. Sturminster Newton Museum Society. Sturminster Newton Parish Council Minutes, 1910 to 1973. Sturminster Newton Town Council. Minute Books of Sturminster Newton Women's Institute. Interview by Technical and Vocational Education Initiative participants (1980s). Arnold Trowbridge. Ian Trowbridge. Vera Upshall. Louise Walters. Fred Weeks (interview by Alan Harrison, October 1996). William Barnes Country Primary School staff. David Williams. Rosemary Wynn.

Chapter 9 was compiled from material submitted by the organisations included.

Index

List of Subscribers

Sturminster Newton Museum Society would like to thank all those whose names
are listed below as well as the subscribers who chose to remain anonymous.
Their support and interest helped make this book possible.

Barbara Abel
Ron Acott
Anne M. Adkins
Mrs S. Agar
Patrick Ager
The Archibald Family

David W. Bacon
Joan Balding
David Banham
Matthew Bartlett
John A. Barbet
Sheila Barnes
Roy Barrett
Stephen Bartlett
Ann & Graham Baseden
Anne Beales
Michael Bean
A. J. Benn
Alan & Judith Bennett
John & Pat Billen
Mr & Mrs David Birt
Erich Bittner
Mr G. Blackmore
Mrs Stella Blackhall
Heather Bogan
Norma Bonnell
John Boulton

David Boulton
Sylvia Boulton
Peter Boxer
W.E.Bradbury
Lyn Brewer
Zilla & Richard Brown
Hannah Louise Brown
Katherine Georgia Brown
Joan & Alan Brown
Jane Bryan
D. K. Bungey
Tony Burnside
Ambrose Bushell
Mr D. Byrne

Mr Bryan Campbell-Down
Linda Carroll
Miss Katie Carter
Gillian R. Carter
Steve Case
John Case
Ray Castell
All At Castle Farm
Wendy Catley
Mr John D. Chilcott
Margaret Clarke
Geoffrey Clacy
Eddie & Win Clarke

Martin Clarke
Roy Clarke
Reginald Walter Cluett
Dorothy & Norman Coles
Elaine Collett
Mrs S. Collett
Nancy Cooke
Graham O. J. Cooke
Michael & Judith Coombe
Sylvia R. Corden
David & Luise Cornes
Betty Cowley
Michelle Cox
Janet Croad
Mrs A. Crocker
Miss Joyce Cundle
Emma Curtis
Matthew Curtis
Mrs Dorothy Curtis

Barbara Daly
B. Danoris
David
Michael S. Davidson
Harry & Gracie Dawes
Sarah Dean
D. A. Dobbins
Leonard Dodson

Patricia Dodson
Andrew Donaldson
Mr Ronald Dorrington
Dorchester Library
Dorset History Centre
Robert Downs
Martin Drake F.R.I.C.S
Mr & Mrs M. Drew
M. S. Drummond
David Durkin

Mrs Doris Easterbrook
Mary Eckardt
Jonathan Eckardt
Peter John Eggs
Peter & Teresa Elkins
John S. Elkins
Stephen John Elkins
Barbara M. Elkins
Joshua Erskine
William Mackenzie Evans
C. L. Eyles
Chris Eyres

Penelope Findlay
Bert Fish
Nigel Foote
Brian Foot
Mr Malcolm J. Ford
Pamela Mary Forward
Carol Foster-Smith
David C. Fox
Terence A. Fox
Victor Fox
Abi Fox
Emma Fox
Kate Fox
Charles S. Fraser
Heather M. Fullarton

Peter Gafney
J. A. & P. R. Gale

Leslie & Doreen Gates
Pat Gee
Christopher George
Mike Gilbert
Professor Geoffrey J. Giles
Dick Gillam
Mrs Violet Goddard
Mrs Hazel Goddard
Steve & Vi Goddard
Leonard Goff
Mrs P. S. Golding
A.K. & M.D. Griffith-Jones
John Grinnell
Malcolm Groves
Constance M. Guttridge
Christine Guy

Olive A. Hall
Eric Hamblin
Miss Vivien Joan Hammond
Mr Philip Lionel Hammond
Kurt Hanson
Kerry Hanson
Alan Hannah
Muriel Harris
Philip Andrew Hart
Mary Harvey
Stephen Harvey
Patsy Haskett
Mary Haskett
Frances Haskett
Jim & Peggy Hatcher
Robert Hatcher
Rosemary Hatcher
Maud Hawkins
Pete Hawkins
J. Haywood
Sally Jane Heavens
Leyla Helvaci
Zahra Helvaci
Gordon, Michelle & Katie Henderson
D. R. & J. M. Hewitson

I. Hewitt
Mrs Angela Hicks
Ronald C. Hill
Mary Hilliam
Ashley Hitchcock
Charles Hollier
Keith & Gillian Honeybun
Jilly & Kenny Hookham-Bassett
Susan Howse
A. A. Hughes
A. R. Hughes
Derek & Myra Hurford (nee Upshall)

Mrs Ruby Joan Inkpen

Les James
Mrs Sheila Jarman
Holly Jarvis
Diana Jose
Elizabeth Annie Joyce
Thelma Joyce (nee Pope)

Violet Kapinski (nee Ingram)
Marie Kittus
Kevin Knapp, Sturminster Newton
    Town Crier

David & Ann Lacey
Samantha Lam
E. A. Lanham
Amanda J. Legg
Trevor Legg
Julie Legg
C. W. Letchford
V. Levens
Mrs Carol Ann Levett
Nigel D. Levy
Linda Margaret Lewis
Jax Lewis
Phil Lines
Paul Litton
Karine Litton

Agatha Loader
Michael Loader
Simon Loader
Jill Loader
Peter Loosmore
Philip Loosmore
Roger Lowman
Philomena Lowman
Lynton Cottage

Jim & Nancy Macfarlane
Mrs Jan Malpass
Kenneth J. Mantock
Ruth Marks
Jack Martin
Sylvia Martin
John Matthews
David & Sylvia May
Robin Mckay
Enid Mercer
Geoff Miller
Carole Miller
Mrs Juliette Mitchell
Simon Moody
Mr & Mrs P. W. Moody
Muriel Moss
Michael Mounch
Anita & Derek Mountain
Hamish & Judy Mountain
Penny Mountain
Mrs Sally Murch

Mike Neville
Jenny Newman
Jessica North
Richard H. Norman

Florence Obee
Carol Odell
Colin Orman
Hayley Orman
Lesley Otter

Lynda Parsons
Tina Parkes
Rosalie Parrott
Caroline Parsons
Sheila & Bob Peacock
Michael Peevor
Mrs Daryl Ann Perry
John & Anne Pidgeon
Sarah Pidgeon
Connor Pidgeon
B. Pidgeon
Eric Piggott
Rosemary Piggott
Poets Corner Café
Elizabeth Preston
Belinda Pring

Jill Rawson
Joan & Bill Rawlings
Mrs P. J. Rawles
Jeremy Read
Philip H. Rhodes
L. Ridout
Mrs E.D.Ring
Mary Robbins
Gwyn E. Rogers
Simon M. Rogers
T. Mark Rogers
Dr A. J. Rogers
Ronald Rolf
Muriel Rooms
David J. Rose
Thomas & Jane Rose Family Society Inc
Sylvia Rose
David Rose
Edmund (Eddie) Rose
Mrs June I. Rose (Cardiff)
Douglas G. Rose
Susannah Louise Ross
Ron Rowland
Phyllis Rowland
Jeanette Russell

Carol Sandall
David Sandall
Clare Sandall
Sarah Sandall
Charlotte Sandall
M. Score
T. Score
Janet Scott-Puttock
John Sedwell
Reginald Sellers
Shaftesbury Library
Rosalind Shaw (nee Danoris)
Sherborne Library
The Sherwood Taylor Family
Olivia Grace Shearer
Sherborne Museum
Freelin Short
Dawn Sidford
Eileen Simpson
Morgan Smith
John A. Smith
C. J. A. Springford
William David Squire
Stalbridge Library
Susan Stanley (nee Upshall)
Tony Stables
Mrs Sheila Staples
Ann (Burt) Stockley
Mr P. Stroud
Sturminster Library
John Sumner

Lily Elizabeth Thorne
John D. Tinsley
Louis Tite
Mrs Betty Tite
Miss E. Tivey
J. P. L. Tory
Yvonne Tribe
Reuben Trowbridge
Arnold Trowbridge
Jo Trowbridge

Mary & Jack Turk

Edward & Vera Upshall
Sheela Upton
Joyce Viner
M. J. Vining
Eric Vining
Joss Vining
Vic & Priscilla Vining

The Wallaces
Ray Walters
Brian Wareham
Liz Warham

Rod & Sylvia Warham
Bryan W. Warland
Robert Weaver
J. K. Webb
Mr H. B. Welch
Fred & Linda Welch
Kenneth J. Westwood
John White
Victor White
Tracy White
Hannah White
Stephanie White
Ruth White
Mary White

Jack Whitehead
The Williams Family
Grace Willis
Muriel Willis
Mike Williams
Michael Williams
David Williams
Margaret Williamson
Roy Willment
Linda Wilton
Harry Woolford
Linda Wort
Vivienne Wordley
Rosemary Wynn